Hidden France

Hidden France

AN INSIDER'S GUIDE TO THE MOST BEAUTIFUL VILLAGES

BRIGITTE TILLERAY

Photographs by Richard Turpin

CASSELL

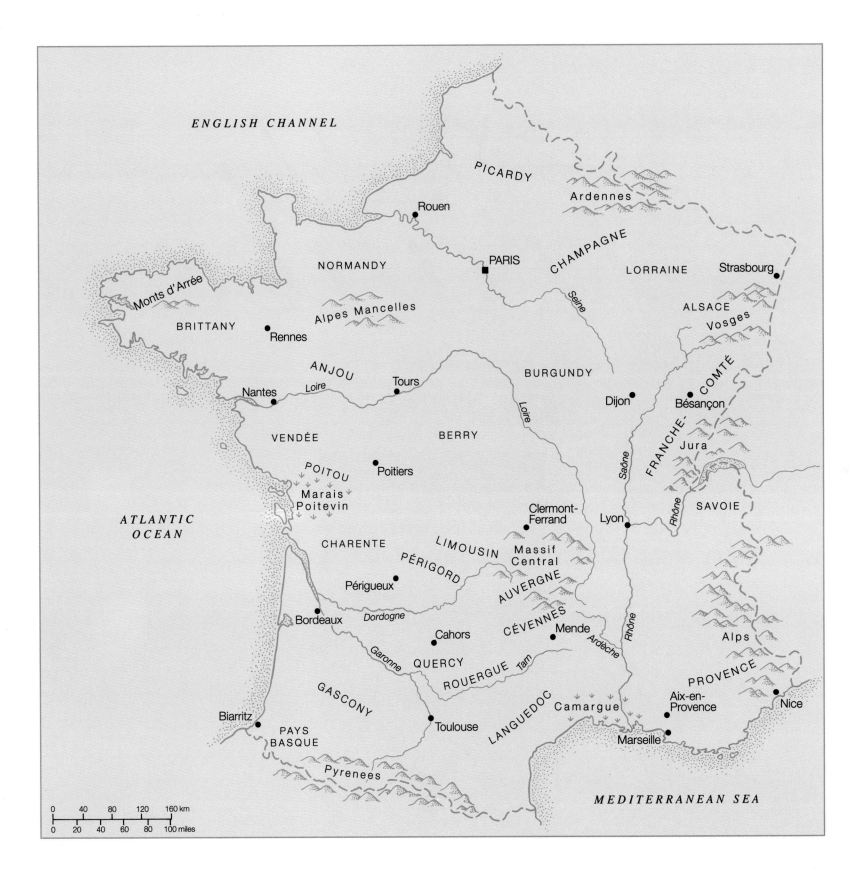

CONTENTS

INTRODUCTION

The church bells strike the last notes of the Angelus, shutters are opening, an exquisite aroma floats from the *boulangerie*. Dressed in black, head down, the tiny figure of a *grand-mère* trots towards the church; a man and his dog push open the door of the *café-tabac*: the French village is awake.

The ritual of French village life is to be found throughout the land, ineffably fighting against the temptations of the nearby towns. The old villagers have never left, but the young are now coming back to preserve or to revive their ancient regional heritage. There is now more life in the winding streets and squares, and pretty flowers brighten doorways from Picardy to the depths of Provence: the era of abandoned villages is over.

Crowning a lonely hill or perched on a mountainside, strung along a quiet coastline or clustered around a church or castle, French villages have managed to keep their regional authenticity. There is no denying that some villages are immediately bewitching; others may appear on first acquaintance to hold no more than a sedate passing interest. But with familiarity comes an understanding of the deeper appeal – a breathtaking setting or striking architecture gratify the senses instantly. The ability of a place to captivate depends not only on the subtle harmony of houses in a street, a beautiful church, an impressive château or a rare architectural detail, but is also governed by its people and their social mores, the peculiarities of local food and wine, the atmosphere of a market place, the climate, colours and perfumes according to the season or the moment.

This book is a journey, a lingering exploration of the diversity of French villages, from Brittany's remote religious communities to the vertiginous *villages perchés* of Provence, discovering the watery delights of the Marais Poitevin and the medieval half-timbered treasures of Alsace. What follows is not a gazetteer but a series of *morceaux choisis*, a genuine *invitation au voyage*.

Frontispiece: *Gordes in the heart of Provence.*

Opposite: *The tiny village of Saint-Floret in the Auvergne.*

NORMANDY

'The scent of my land is held in an apple, I bite into it with my eyes closed, pretending I am in a green orchard. The tall grass smells of the sun and the sea.'

This is how the author Lucie Delarue Mardrus spoke of her native Normandy, this sensuous region where, in the mind's eye, the girls' cheeks are as red as the apples, and where sun and rain work in harmony to confer opulence and beauty.

To colour this lush land you need two crayons: a blue one to draw the sea, and a green one for the land, this rich pastureland of meadows and *bocage* – a chequerboard landscape where, in the spring, the shades of green are endless. No grass is as rich as the grass of Normandy.

It is not surprising that the region has always been an inspiration for artists, among them Jongkind, Courbet, Corot and, above all, Eugène Boudin, who was born in the picturesque fishing harbour of Honfleur, and became the precursor of Claude Monet. Both Boudin and Monet were fascinated by the immensity of the Normandy skies and the visual after-effects of the rain on the spring and summer landscape.

In May, for a short while, two more colours are added to the palette, as the pear, apple and cherry-tree orchards, together with the sweet-smelling hawthorn, are bedecked with ephemeral blossom in white and pink, deepening to red as the fruit ripens in autumn. From the Calville and Reinette used to complement poultry and make *tarte aux pommes*, to the tiny cider apple, the ultimate fruit of the region is its apples.

To add to this beautiful landscape, there is an immense collection of glorious farmhouses, ancient historical cities and a multitude of traditionally structured villages, complete with stone churches, large manor houses and *maisons de maître* – substantial squarish homes often occupied by doctors or notaries – and a shopping street with half-timbered façades. The region's natural materials such as wood, stone and straw have been crafted together with brick into a distinctive style of architecture, perpetuated over centuries by master builders. In Upper Normandy, the half-timbering known as *colombage* is prevalent, the heavy exposed beams filled with wattle and daub or a pattern of soft red bricks. In Seine-Maritime, flint is used a great deal, often with brick surrounds for door and window openings. Once you cross the river Seine, the style alters. First the *colombage* again, but with thatched roofs and, around the fashionable resorts of Deauville and Cabourg, extravagant homes with immense roofs, and balconies off every bedroom. Then, towards Caen and the south, limestone and granite appear, with roofs made of slate or blue schist. The style of the churches is as diverse as the rest of the architecture: in the north, the roofs

(page 8) *In the heart of the Pays de Bray, in the most easterly reaches of Normandy, the timbered houses of Gerberoy are painted in soft shades of blue, giving a distinctive touch in this cradle of Impressionism.*

and bell towers are often covered with slate over a solid stone building; in Honfleur, the gem of the Normandy coastline, the church of Sainte-Catherine is made entirely of wood. Travelling further west, towards the Cotentin Peninsula, the straight stone spires brood over the villages, austere and indomitable.

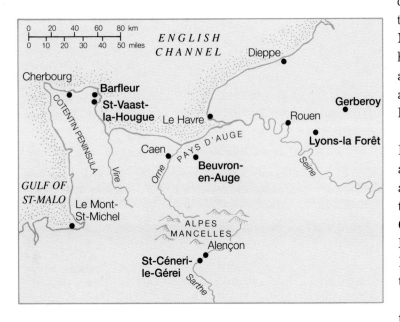

In this fruitful land, where cream, cheese and wholesome farm produce are on the table at every meal, where cider is the only conceivable thirst quencher and calvados the remedy of all pains and sorrows, the folk are sturdy. Farmers or sailors, they have an evident physical strength inherited from their Viking ancestors and stay faithful to their traditions. Normandy is a region where tradition has never died and therefore will never need to be reinvented.

The whole of Normandy officially stretches from Picardy to Mont-Saint-Michel and from the tip of the Cherbourg peninsula to the doors of Chartres and Paris, an area so vast that it has been divided into enclaves called *pays*. So, people do not refer about themselves as Normans but as 'du Pays de Caux', 'du Pays d'Auge', 'du Pays du Contentin', 'du Pays

d'Ouche'... And if the people of Upper and Lower Normandy argue their true Norman stock, it becomes even more complicated when you reach the Pays de Bray. Is this still Normandy or is it already Picardy? Some will say it is Beauvaisis, as it is so near the city of Beauvais, which boasts the tallest Gothic cathedral in France. But the houses are built in true Norman style and the nearby town of Neufchatel-en-Bray produces Normandy's heart-shaped Neufchatel cheese. So, forget the arguments started by William the Conqueror, and visit Gerberoy, in a sleepy corner of the Pays de Bray.

At the end of the nineteenth century, Impressionist painters such as Monet, Sisley and Pissarro ate, danced, loved and worked among the water meadows, riverside cafés and tree-clad banks of the Seine, the Marne or the Oise. Further north, in the countryside of the Pays de Bray, their friend and other disciple of Impressionism, Henri Le Sidaner, succumbed to the charms of Gerberoy.

The village had been torn and ransacked through the Middle Ages by the atrocities of the Hundred Years War, the plague and a huge fire. The houses were ruins, the medieval walls overgrown. Was it the bucolic name of the place – the evocation of royal cornfields and haystacks – or the picturesque aspect of this village which enchanted the artist? Whatever the inspiration, friends and handymen soon joined Henri Le Sidaner who had started to restore the village to its former glory.

Today, surrounded by a shaded walk, the picture-book village is a charming medley of houses. Flowers of all kinds burst out of garden walls and sprout beside the paved streets. The attractive century-old garden created by Le Sidaner remains, just as he painted it. The whole village is a joyous fantasy of architectural rural styles where stonework mixes with local bricks next to softly painted timber frames and

Summer ripeness in Gerberoy (opposite): *the brightly coloured flowers and an ancient wisteria add to the charm of a cosy cottage and its walled gardens in this peaceful corner of the village.*

pale ochre wattle and daub. Follow the winding streets, admire the naïve stone head on the porch of a house in the Grande Rue, amble towards the communal well, or step under the elegant stone archway which leads to the ramparts and you will understand why Gerberoy, not too impaired by the trappings of tourism, still attracts artists and nature lovers.

Almost halfway between the Pays de Bray and the city of Rouen, hides the woodland village of Lyons-la-Forêt. Take a stroll along any of the paths of the immense forest which surrounds Lyons-la-Forêt, and you will be walking in Europe's largest beech wood, where the dukes of Normandy once hunted. Some specimens here are over 300 years old. If, by lunchtime, the walk has sharpened your appetite, you can eat an excellent duck with fresh cherries at the local *hostellerie*, a beamed seventeenth-century building standing in the square of this classical Norman village.

Lyons-la-Forêt's circular centre was built inside the ramparts of a twelfth-century château erected by Henry I of England, but it claims an even more ancient past, since excavations have uncovered the remains of a Roman theatre. The focal point must be the covered market. Its immense roof with dormer windows shelters an art and crafts gallery, while underneath a busy country market is held three times a week.

Lyons is a place of great charm, where half-timbered houses mix with red brick, and pantiles have given way to slate roofs. The rue d'Enfer is lined with a magnificent ensemble of seventeenth- and eighteenth-century timbered homes, the exceptional craftsmanship showing in the roofs, with their central turrets and rows of dormer windows crowned by ornate ceramic finials. In this region where it so often rains, small roofs run over the windows to deflect rain from the window frame, mixing the functional with the picturesque. Cross the river to look at the twelfth-century church with its handsome

geometric shingling. The whole setting of the village is peaceful, with country gardens running into orchards all the way to the river Lieure. This was the setting which inspired Flaubert to write *Madame Bovary* and where, a few years later, from his ancient house set in the hilly rue d'Enfer, Maurice Ravel composed his intricate suite for piano, 'Le Tombeau de Couperin'.

A short walk away from Lyons you will find the Abbaye de Mortemer, whose twelfth- and thirteenth-century Cistercian buildings are now a museum set in a park.

Travelling south-west, the countryside develops into some of the finest in Normandy. After the plain of Alençon, the landscape changes softly into rolling hills and valleys, then to high rocky points: les Alpes Mancelles. The hills are covered with woods, carpeted with unusual plants, massive ferns, and, in the autumn, wild mushrooms. Coypu have made their home here, trout fill the streams, and even

The huge covered market of Lyon-la-Forêt (above) spans the whole square. On market days, flowers and country produce are on sale under the arches, while in the adjacent cafés and hostelries, cattlemen and horse dealers play cards and dominoes in the same warm bustling atmosphere that inspired Flaubert.

Through an old gateway in Gerberoy (opposite), flowers spill over the pavements and clamber up house walls. Houses here differ in size and style according to their age, and stone and local brick have been used side by side with Norman timbering.

a few crayfish still hide under the rocks. The small fields are edged with luscious hedgerows. From the hills there are distant views over quaint hamlets and wild orchards half hidden in the folds of the countryside. Riding is a joy among the quiet country lanes of the Suisse Normande, as the area is known, and many of the large, isolated farms are stud farms, breeders of many prizewinners at Longchamp and Chantilly.

A few kilometres away from the city of Alençon, centre for the fine needlepoint lace known as *point d'Alençon*, is a picturesque village standing on a promontory by a meander of the river Sarthe. It is Saint-Céneri-le-Gérei.

Saint-Céneri bears the name of the Italian monk who discovered the site in the seventh century. Joined by other monks, he built a monastery at the very place where the church now stands. The village, which has inspired such artists as Courbet and Corot, was built mainly around the bridge, between church and château. The tiled and slate-hung houses are beautifully kept, with pretty gardens hanging in terraces along the river. They were once the home of the many artisans and hemp weavers who lived in Saint-Céneri. From the top of the village you can enjoy the view down on to the charming fourteenth-century chapel built over a mono-lithic stone on which the saint used to lay and pray. It is today a place of pilgrimage.

It would be a crime to go to the Normandy resorts of Deauville and Trouville without visiting the rolling countryside behind the stylish beaches. The Pays d'Auge is a gracious green land with soft horizons and a fecund artistic past, is rich in immense stud farms and handsome châteaux such as Crèvecoeur-en-Auge and, the most charming of them all, Saint-Germain-de-Livet.

This is cider country. Follow the Route du Cidre along which irises sprout curiously from thatched roofs and stop at a *ferme-auberge* or a

A misty morning transforms the leafy landscape of Saint-Céneri-le-Gérei into a scene worthy of Corot. The old bridge spans the river Sarthe to link the two parts of this pretty village.

As was common, the downstairs rooms of this farmhouse in Beuvron-en-Auge in the Pays d'Auge (right) *open straight on to the garden, to improve the air flow if the chimney started smoking. The upper walls of timber-frame farmhouses like these are covered with slates to protect the walls from rain. Although early on wattle and daub was mostly used, the introduction of brick infilling* (below) *made the walls more weatherproof.*

country café for charcuterie and local cheeses: Camembert, Pont-l'Evêque and Livarot, served with jugs of cider poured straight from the barrel. The apples from which cider is made are unpleasantly sour, but make a welcoming drink and an even more heart-warming tipple when distilled into calvados. There are the panoramic views of the *pays* from the square at Beaumont-en-Auge, a profoundly rural small town with tall slate-faced houses, handsome eighteenth-century buildings and an interesting art gallery offering the work of local artists. Not far away is Beuvron-en-Auge, which is a symphony of timber framing.

Once an important seigneury and archidiocese of the Pays d'Auge, the village now stretches along two roads and around an elliptic square dominated by a huge covered market. Unfortunately Beuvron's market days have gone and the *halles* now shelter antique and craft shops and an unmissable restaurant where the

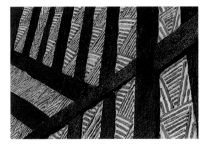

The allée de la Catouille in Beuvron-en-Auge (right) *leads into a sunny yard surrounded by modest timbered cottages and a larger house supported by massive angle posts.*

which has been heavily restored in the nineteenth century, is plain with a good collection of crystal chandeliers. On the outskirt, a handsome manor house, Le Manoir de Hocquartet, hides in the folds of the hills and, on the north side, way up in the woods, there is a small chapel with commanding views across rich pastureland. Beyond lie the marshes of the river Dives where it runs towards the sea at Cabourg.

The tall, hooded roof of this ochre-coloured manor house (left) *typifies the region's architecture. Its gardens lead through rich grasses and meadowsweet to the river Beuvronette.*

Normandy specialities are genuine even if they have been prepared for years by a woman who originates from Alsace.

The back alleys bear charming names such as rue de la Catouille – Tickling Lane in Norman patois. You will buy groceries in an *épicerie* which has kept all the charms of yesteryear and gather the news of the day at the barber-shop which is also the local café. It stands at the corner of the square by a stream, once the home of beavers: la Beuvronette. The little river trickles through the surrounding water meadows and under the small garden bridges built at the back of the village towards a magnificent sixteenth-century ochre-coloured manor house. Its exquisite carved timbering representing demonic faces contrasts sharply with the owner's choice of romantic hand-crocheted curtains at the windows.

Other reminders of the medieval outlook of the village have disappeared and the church,

Marking the western limits of Normandy, the Cotentin Peninsula sticks up like a thumb into La Manche, the English Channel. At its tip, the village of Barfleur seems to emerge from the sea. Here, the villagers and fishermen live their daily life constantly fighting the insurgence of modern tourist developments. A look at the small granite port at low tide, when the fishing boats are softly tilting on the seaweed bed, makes one realize how right they are to cling to their traditional ways.

What was once a large rural town has become a village of a few hundred inhabitants, mainly fishermen, who live in a very tight community. This does not mean that visitors are not welcomed, but they will have to be content with the simple pleasures that the area has to offer: a walk along the quay and, later, when the boats have returned loaded with fish, mussels and coquilles Saint-Jacques, a coffee and a glass of calvados at the local café while the *patronne* cooks kilos of mussels and has her own closely kept recipe for soused herring.

Walks through and around Barfleur are endlessly rewarding, as the village changes colour and mood with every tide, every season, every time of the day.

Fishing boats await high tide to leave the quayside at Saint-Vaast-la-Hougue, on the northern tip of the Cotentin peninsula. A stronghold against the English during the Hundred Years War, the harbour is fortified on one side. It has a long jetty and a tiny chapel dedicated to the fishing community.

The whole village is dominated by the church of Saint-Nicolas, a solid Norman building which stands at the mouth of the harbour. A little *chemin de ronde* will take you around the church, past the handsome presbytery, towards cottages built among the rocks. All you can hear amid this salty landscape is the shrieking of the seagulls busy cracking mussel shells against the rock before they quickly eat them. Then, past the house once inhabited by artist Paul Signac, a Post-Impressionist who, with Seurat and others, started the Pointillist movement, you reach the busy quay lined with handsome Napoleon III houses. There, even if the boats have left for the

Barfleur (opposite), *the historic harbour from which the Norman Conquest was launched, is to this day the most unspoilt fishing village of this part of the coast.*

day, you will be able to watch men tending their nets or lobster pots; jovial retired fishermen, they will entertain you with local jokes or, if you are lucky, give you one of their secret recipes for fish.

Finally you will reach the main street, rue Saint-Thomas. At the baker, buy *un pain plié*, a cottage loaf folded in the shape of Napoleon's hat, and admire the solid seventeenth- and eighteenth-century houses built when fortunes were flourishing in the area. The street leads to small alleys such as cour Sainte-Catherine, with higgledy-piggledy cottages reached by large stone steps. Doorways are made of great arched granite blocks and everywhere in late summer is a riot of wild fuchsia and blue hydrangea.

Through the courtyard, a stone archway leads back to the entrance of the port, and it is from there that you can take in the whole charm of Barfleur. Particular to the village are the blue schist roofs, the tiles cemented to protect the roof from the mean winter easterlies. The unusual ceramic roof ridges, called *faitages*, which run along the entire length of the roof, are still hand-made in the village by a ceramicist who believes in tradition. Of ancient origin, the *faitage* is made of brown, cobalt or green round tiles edged by a spike in the shape of buttons, fleur-de-lis or lace. To crown the peak of the roof are the *épis de faitage*, masterpieces of care and artistry in the form of birds, animals, or small men with top hats and fat tummies.

Not far from Barfleur is the bustling fishing port of Saint-Vaast-la-Hougue, which has acquired a fine reputation for the excellence of its food and wine shops, and especially its oysters. At the end of the road, in the picturesque village of Le Vast, you can watch the local baker making *pain à l'ancienne* in a wood oven. On Sundays people travel from far afield to buy a brioche made with fine Normandy butter to eat for tea with redcurrant or blackcurrant jam.

BRITTANY

———

'**K**ant bro, kant giz, kant parrez, kant iliz': 'a hundred areas, a hundred customs, a hundred parishes and a hundred churches' is how the people of Brittany refer to their country in the Breton language.

This massive headland, almost detached from the rest of France, stands proud and stubborn like its people, diverse and distinctive like the landscape, mystical like the Celtic heritage and the language. First, there is the coast, dramatically rocky on the northern Côte d'Armor while soft and balmy in the south, around Morbihan. Inland, forests and moorlands covered with honey-scented gorse and heather retain the charm and mysteries of the region's legends, the chapels, the calvaries, the megalithic menhirs and dolmens. There are ancient stone-built fishing ports and elegant cities like Rennes and Quimper and, at the same time the addition of modern houses, handsome and so distinct from the rest of France with their whitewashed walls, slate roofs and stone dormer windows.

But above all, there are the people of Brittany. Tough and resilient, they have crossed the oceans, fished the seas and dug the arid soil; some speak French, others Breton but, in the end, they all unite to retain the traditions of the land. The most significant traditions include the *pardons*, massive yearly religious meetings, with the Celtic music of bagpipes and of accordions. These celebrate the local patron saint and are an opportunity to see Breton women in their traditional embroidered dresses and elaborate lace headdresses. The food, despite the richness of the soil and the sea, remains simple and sustaining. For the Breton, food is like life or religion: a no-nonsense affair. Among the staples is the large and featherlight buckwheat pancake, *galette*, together with pork produce, good vegetables and three sweet specialities: the *far*, a rather heavy eggy pudding with prunes, the *gâteau breton*, a moist and buttery cake and the *kuoing amman*, a scrumptious caramelized yeast pastry oozing with butter. As in Normandy, cider is a favourite drink. It is often drunk from a *bolée*, a ceramic cup, rather than a glass. Here, the apple eau-de-vie is called lambig.

'Stone', said the nineteenth-century philosopher and historian Ernest Renan, 'seems to be the natural symbol of the Celtic races. They are as immutable as the undying rock.' Renan was born and educated at Tréguier, on the northern rocky coastline of Brittany. The region is a magnificent jagged cornice of granite, mostly pink, where the savage winter sea shows its force, and where faith and tradition seem the safest refuge against the elements.

At Trégastel and Ploumanach, the rocks which scatter the seashore have been sculpted by the waves into curious shapes and forms, and so

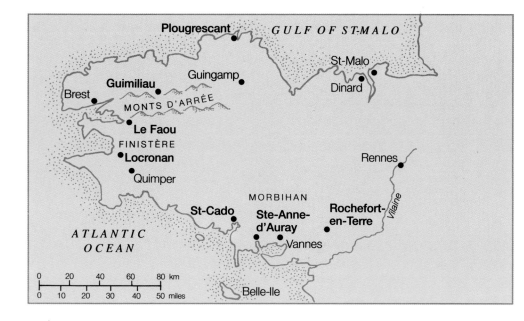

naturally have picturesquely descriptive names – La Tête de Mort, the skull; Le Tire-bouchon, the corkscrew; Le Tas de Crêpes, the pile of pancakes. Along this amazing coastline is Plougrescant, its cottage built between two enormous rocks. This house seems to have become the symbol of the area. It stands there as if the rocks had suddenly grown, like magic trees, to protect the fisherman's abode from the inhospitable surge of waves. In the surrounding garden wild mignonette grows among dry-stone walls. Around, hundreds of small islets covered with seaweed so gorged with goodness that you feel like bathing among it. The seaweed industry is in full progress in Brittany and different kinds are increasingly used by chefs who are keen to experiment with the natural ingredients of the region.

Do not leave Plougrescant without visiting the chapel of Saint-Gonery, with its leaning steeple and, inside, two beautiful alabaster carvings from Nottingham, a testimony of the artistic contacts between Brittany and Britain in the Middle Ages. The chapel's original wood panelling is still intact; painted in blue and red with flowers and crosses, it is an astonishing

piece of popular art, with a God who creates the sun, a moon with a human face, plants and animals.

Stone and religion are intricately linked in Brittany, and from St Pol-de-Léon, just along the coast from Plougrescant, inland across the district of Léon, can be found the most extraordinary of all Christian architecture in France: the *enclos paroissiaux*. These elaborate enclosures, all built on more or less the same pattern, are a ring of granite walls around a chapel or church, a calvary and an ossuary. The entrance is a highly decorated gateway called an *arc de triomphe*. Parishes would attempt to outbid each other in the ostentation of the carvings in their *enclos*, to reflect the wealth and religious devotion of the *seigneurs* and cloth weavers in the sixteenth and seventeenth centuries when they were built, and the result is a bizarre yet strangely pleasing mixture of the religious and the profane.

Among the most ancient *enclos* are the incredibly ornate Saint-Thégonnec and, just to its south, Guimiliau. The *enclos* here teems with granite figures, two hundred alone on the calvary, depicting fifteen episodes from the life of Christ. Some are naïve in their workmanship, while others, such as those in the seventeen scenes from the Passion, are full of expression.

A crooked wall and a crooked spire: the tipsy effect of the Gonery chapel at Plougrescant is the result of warping in its centuries-old timber frame.

Along the Brest estuary, the village of Le Faou (right) was once a bustling river port. Today, it is the gateway to the incomparable Crozon peninsula, a breathtaking wild headland between Brest and Douarnenez.

As well as the 200 carved figures adorning its calvary, the church at Guimiliau has a beautifully carved south porch (left), dominated by the statue of its patron saint, Saint Miliau.

The south-facing porch of the church, with its adjacent ossuary, holds a handsome figure of Saint Miliau, a local healer.

The next stop will be Finistère, the land's end of France. This western tip of the country resembles a beast, fangs bared, the open mouth about to bite at the ocean. There is something very special about standing on the very tip of one's own country. Pride? Emotion? At the Cap de la Chèvre, on the Crozon peninsula, you feel it. People walk and handglide over moorland carpeted with moss and heather, surrounded by endless views over the coastline. To the left, the bay of Brest opens up into long estuaries: Plougastel, Daoulas and Le Faou.

Le Faou was once a busy port, shipping wood felled from the nearby forests. The quays are still here along the river, a reminder of how busy it must have been, and among more modern buildings there remain medieval houses with their slate-clad corbelling. The tall seventeenth-century church has a bell-shaped steeple called the *lanternon*. From the top you can see the ancient Monts d'Arrée, gentle crests on the eastern horizon. Swivel to the right and there is the fishing port of Douarnenez, where sardines have been canned for two hundred years and, just behind, in a natural amphi-theatre made by the Porzay hills, the village of Locronan. A uniquely preserved centre for weavers built out of grey granite, Locronan is also the most ancient pilgrimage venue of Brittany.

The story of Locronan starts with Ronan, a monk who came from Ireland in the fifth century, to live a holy life in the community at Finistère. Every day the monk walked barefoot for 5 km around the monastery and, to honour the saint, a silent procession takes place on the same path once a year, in July. This is the

Fifteen centuries have elapsed since the Irish monk, Ronan, founded Locronan (below), nestling in the natural amphitheatre of the Porzay hills.

Troménie, from *tro minihy* which means, in the Breton language, 'tour of the monastery'. It is one of many pilgrimages, known as *pardons*, which enables the devout Bretons to celebrate their saints and pray together as a community. On such days, the women dress in black or in beautifully embroidered traditional costumes, wearing the magnificent lace headdress which varies in height and shape across the region. The best known must be the *coiffe bigoudène*, a tall fluted headdress, impeccably starched, with long lace ribbons at the back, so faithfully represented in the drawings of twentieth-century Breton artist, René-Yves Creston.

Along the ancient route, the pious will halt at twelve points, where relics and representations of saints are displayed. One of them is the cross of Keben. Legend relates that a washerwoman, too busy to stop working when the mortal remains of Ronan went by, had the misfortune of injuring the horns of one of the oxen pulling the saint's bier. She was never forgiven and even today traditionalists pass Keben's halt without crossing themselves. The whole story of the original procession is carved on the exquisite pulpit in Locronan's church, a fifteenth-century jewel of granite architecture unfortunately deprived, today, of its steeple. It is in the adjoining chapel of Le Pénity that Ronan was laid to rest and where the devout come to pray to their saint.

Both church and chapel stand on a large cobbled square surrounded by solid houses of exceptional architecture. They were built at a time when, for a hundred years, until the middle of the eighteenth century, the area prospered with the weaving of *lokornans*, large canvas sails destined for the warships of the French fleet. The elaborate roofs of these cloth merchants' houses have heavy cornices, large dormer windows and solid chimney-stacks, similar to those of priories in western Brittany. In 1924, by which time the traveller had become tourist, the roofs which did not have dormer windows were fitted with those taken from the old hospital of nearby Quimper, creating complete architectural harmony around the square. Today, many of the houses are occupied by artisans and cafés, and one would need a lot of willpower to resist the moist *gâteau breton* or warm *kuoing amman* sold at the *boulangerie* in the afternoon.

In the back alleys, the more modest weavers' cottages, surrounded by pretty gardens, are a further reminder of the source of the town's wealth – local tradition, as recounted at the museum and the Maison des Artisans, attributes

The Celtic bell of Locronan church (left) *rings out to summon pilgrims on the festive day of the Troménie, the most ancient religious gathering in Brittany.*

this, too, to Ronan: it is said that watching a spider at work on her web inspired him to introduce weaving as the villagers' livelihood.

A few kilometres inland, Rochefort-en-Terre is set on a rocky outcrop. This picturesque village was originally a large fortress built by the powerful barons of Malestroit. They built it as a defence position, hard by the fort of Elven, at the entrance to the city of Vannes. The towers of Elven are still one of the most imposing medieval edifices of the western world.

Of the fortress of Rochefort-en-Terre, only a gateway remains, leading into this exquisitely kept village. Laid out according to the traditional medieval plan, there is a long main street leading to the château, with alleyways on both sides of this main axis. From the top end, there is a magnificent view on the wooded valley of Gueuzon and the river Arz. In summer the village bursts with geraniums, a tradition started by the American artist Alfred Klots, in 1911. He also restored the château with material from the seventeenth-century Keralio manor house near Muzillac. A café is named after this foreign philanthropist and artists continue to be attracted to this charming floriferous village. Underneath this floral riot of pink and crimson, or during the winter months when the flowers have been put away, the houses of Rochefort-en-Terre are pure examples of the excellent stonework and delicate craftsmanship of the region. Ornate pediments adorn doorways and windows, turrets with corbelling sprout from houses and hostelries built during the fifteenth to seventeenth centuries.

Inland from Vannes and the Gulf of Morbihan lies Rochefort-en-Terre, overlooked by the rocky Landes de Lanvaux (left). The arched doorway (right) in the place du Puits is typical of the local architecture, and the well which gives the square its name was still in use at the beginning of the twentieth century.

A medley of ancient houses at a street corner in Rochefort-en-Terre, with attic windows and ornate signs adding to the charm. Cascades of pelargoniums enliven the old flagstones and stonework throughout the summer, and wild flowers have seeded themselves in the carved base of a turret in the place du Puits. The adjacent dormer windows have elaborately carved tops.

Returning towards the sea and the fortified medieval city of Vannes with its solid ramparts, cobbled streets and timbered buildings, you will discover Morbihan, the most southern part of Brittany. There, the sea has bitten into the land, leaving a coastline of fjords, called *loc'hs*, and islands. The climate is soft enough to allow the growth of cacti, palm trees and mimosa, and life is almost entirely devoted to boating and the life of the sea.

The Gulf of Morbihan starts from the picturesque peninsula of Rhuys, where Abélard tried to forget Héloise and where the Château de Suscinio, summer residence of the Dukes of Brittany, proudly stands facing the ocean. The gulf stretches to the large commercial port of Lorient, named after its main commerce when, in the seventeenth and eighteenth centuries, vessels left the Brittany coast for the Orient in search of spices and other exotic commodities. In the nearby cidatel of Port-Louis, the Musée de la Compagnie des Indes describes, in full and fascinating detail, the heroic exploits of the Western French fleet.

The seascape of Morbihan is dotted with a multitude of small islands, some so wild and small that they are the domain of seabirds and crustaceans. Others are inhabited, as is the case of the picturesque Ile aux Moines. It can only be reached by boat and it is a joy to amble between the thatched cottages festooned with roses, honeysuckle and wild vine on a stretch of land where no car is allowed.

The coastal region of Carnac and Quiberon is opulent and fashionably frequented by owners of large yachts. The food follows the mood and, in the best-known restaurants, fish soup is served under a featherlight crust of pastry, clams flirt with *ris de veau* – the most delicate of offals, and local turbot is laced with an exquisite Muscadet sauce.

Further along the coast, the region has kept its wild character and identity. Close to Auray,

The ramparts of the medieval city of Vannes are skirted by a sweep of slate roofs on the old wash-houses. These remarkably preserved lavoirs *would for centuries have been the seat of local gossip, as the women gathered not only to do their washing but to swap news, greet neighbours and glean information.*

at the head of a *loc'h* is Sainte-Anne-d'Auray, a renowned place of devotion with a miraculous fountain. The old quarter and fishing port of Saint-Goustan, with steep, entangled streets, boasts a laudable museum which describes the bygone life of the local fishing community. On Sundays, when, towards midday, the bells of the seventeenth-century church ring the end of the mass, it is hard to resist the lure of the ancient *auberges*. There, everyone enters into the serious ceremonial of Sunday lunch. Large families meet over a meal which can last up to four hours, ignoring the running about of the children, talking animatedly over good cider, pungent wine and delicious food which, whether plain or sophisticated, is eaten seriously, almost religiously. This will be, of course, the only meal of the day except for a light supper of cold buckwheat *galettes* eaten in a bowlful of *lait ribot*, buttermilk.

Further west still, past the megaliths of Kerzhero, around which children dance holding hands, is the totally unspoilt estuary of the river Etel, facing the large island of Belle-Ile. Every seaman is well aware of the fatal maelstrom which stretches across the entrance of the estuary, known as the barrage d'Etel; a complex whirlpool of currents so strong that a bore rolls up the river with every high tide. Follow the water towards the wooded countryside of Locoal-Mendon to reach the tiny village of Belz and the islet of Saint-Cado.

At high tide, Saint-Cado can only be reached by a footpath built by the saint who evangelized the area. Son of the Prince of Glamorgan, he came to this corner of Brittany between the fifth and seventh centuries, chased from his homeland, like so many other British monks, by the Saxon invaders.

A great peace exudes from this small oyster-farming community. At the centre of a mossy village green, with peaceful views over the sea from every corner, stands the chapel. Appearing

almost to float, it is naïve, simple, Romanesque and disturbingly romantic. Inside, there is a square granite font-stone, an uncarved under-croft and a simple wooden statue of Saint-Cado. Only the altar is decorated, with seasonal flowers from the island. Outside, the air is perfumed with the exquisite aroma of wild herbs blended with the ozonic odour of seaweed and of the distant waves. The gently carved coastline and the row of fishermen's cottages on the quay of Belz across the water, reminds one of the Brittany which inspired Paul Gauguin. 'When my clogs tread on the granite of Brittany,' he said, 'I hear the soft, muted solidity that I constantly seek when I paint.'

The simple granite houses, each with their lean-to known as a *penty*, that he captured so often on canvas, have kept their character, the grey stone or whitewash stark against the blue of doors and shutters. Often, inside, if the house still belongs to a fisherman, wooden partitions and ceilings will be painted with the same dark green paint used for the boats. A sense of economy? More likely an ancestral superstition, like so many others which surround the lives of men who daily risk their lives at sea, and on whom Brittany continues to depend.

According to legend, the tiny island of Saint-Cado (opposite), off the Morbihan coast, was only linked to the mainland when Cado, a son of the Prince of Glamorgan, made a pact with the Devil to build a causeway. As the tide goes out the source of the main activity on Saint-Cado is revealed: oyster beds (above). Packed in flat sacks laid on wooden platforms around the island, the oysters are sold by fishermen from their cottage doorways.

THE PAYS DE LOIRE

By the time the Loire reaches Orléans, catching the reflections of the lovely châteaux built for the kings of France, this great river has already travelled a long way. From its source near Le Puy in the Massif Central far to the south, it has run through the cornfields of the Petite Beauce into the Brenne and the Sologne, France's most noble shooting and hunting ground, to bathe *le jardin de la France*. This region with the softest of climates subtly divides the north of France from the south, and even the weathermen define their daily forecast by '*au nord de la Loire… au sud de la Loire…*'.

The valley of the Loire reaches its epitome in the spring, and even the wines seem to have a vernal quality, the light fruitiness of Saumur-Champigny or Saint-Nicolas-de-Bourgueil. Like the wines of Chinon or Vouvray, they seem to be intimately linked to the quality of the soil. Vines such as Cabernet franc, Sauvignon and Gamay seem ideally suited to the mix of sand, clay and tufa of the valley – the white wine of Cour-Cheverny originates from vines planted by François I in 1518. And, as you follow the river downstream towards its wide estuary, in the Pays de Nantes, you find Muscadet and Gros Plant, natural accompaniments to the seafood of the Atlantic coast.

Joan of Arc led the French to victory against the English at Orléans in 1429, and Chinon and Blois witnessed other bloody battles during the Hundred Years War, but the Loire valley is cherished above all as the land of poets, from Charles d'Orléans to Pierre Ronsard. Here, in the cradle of the French Renaissance, queens planted magnificent rose gardens and the French court made its royal progress in a voluptuous spirit of enjoyment.

The Pays de Loire is an illustrious cortège of regal châteaux, from Chambord, the monumental hunting lodge of François I believed to have been partly designed by Leonardo da Vinci, to the graceful architecture of Blois, Amboise and Azay-le-Rideau. Chenonceau was *le château des dames*, summer residence of, in turn, Diane de Poitiers, Mary Stuart and Catherine de' Medici, while Cheverny's formal *jardins à la française* are among the finest in the whole of France.

The Loire is also a region of historic abbeys. At the Benedictine abbey of Saint-Benoît-sur-Loire, the Lutheran doctrines of the Reformation were embraced and at Fontevraud lies Henry II, founder of the English Plantagenet dynasty, with his queen, Eleanor of Aquitaine, and their eldest son, Richard the Lionheart.

Among all this splendour are to be found numerous villages of charm and grace. Their houses are solidly built out of the local limestone, and if none of them compares with the grandeur of the neighbouring châteaux, there is, here and there, a turret, a mullioned window, a

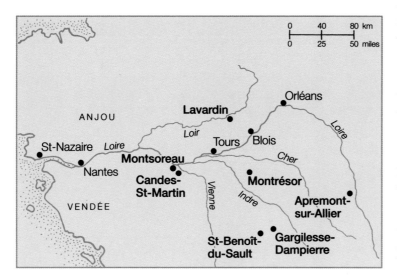

(page 36) *The peace of a summer afternoon by the river Indrois, at Montrésor. The harmonious village is a soft mixture of sandstone and deep russet tiled roofs. The collégiale, the old ruined fort and the opulent château dominate the houses, many of them surviving from the fifteenth and sixteenth centuries.*

carved lintel, to show an appreciation of the finer things. The Pays de Loire is where the purest French is spoken, and the elegant mixture of wine-makers' *maisons vigneronnes*, country gentlemen's residences and Louis Philippe mansions, all set amid pretty gardens and carefully tended *potagers*, reflects the essence of French taste.

A step away from Chinon and the Abbey of Fontevraud is La Devinière, birthplace of François Rabelais, the sixteenth-century monk and writer who, through his epic tales of Pantagruel and Gargantua, has become the personification of burlesque gourmandise. But, behind the creation of such boisterously larger-than-life characters lay the mind of a humanist and ecclesiastic whose favourite place of meditation was nearby Candes-Saint-Martin.

Set at the confluence of the Loire and the Vienne, Candes-Saint-Martin and its surroundings seem to combine all the qualities which characterize the communities of the region: the fine grass sloping towards the river, the sandy beaches uncovered in summer when the water is low, the magnificent ensemble of local stone and slate with which church, château and houses are built. The names of the pristine cobbled streets, such as rue des Pêcheurs and

rue des Mariniers, are reminders of the time when fishing and navigation played an important role in the region's economy. The older houses are opulent, but towards the top of the village are still some good examples of the troglodyte homes which figure in the literature of Rabelais.

The soft limestone of the region lends itself to natural erosion and human excavation, and these cave dwellings have long been a curiosity of the area. Perfectly insulated from wind and sun, the inhabitants can claim their walls are some ninety million years old. Smoke can often be seen spiralling from between rows of vines, where chimneys have been channelled up through the cliffs, and from spring onwards, creeping vines mingle with cascades of nasturtiums, pelargoniums and petunias around brightly painted doors in the cliff face.

The nineteenth-century French novelist, Alexandre Dumas, put Montsoreau, just across the Vienne, on the literary map when his novel, *La Dame de Monsoreau*, followed the publication of *La Reine Margot* in 1846. The novel was based on the tragic ending of the illicit love affair in 1579 between Françoise de Mirador, spouse of Comte Charles de Chambes de Montsoreau, and Bussy d'Amboise. Having learnt about his young wife's indiscretion, the intrepid and jealous 30-year-old count forced her to fix a rendezvous with her lover at the Château de Coutancière, on the opposite bank of the Loire. After a chivalrous fight which cost the life of fourteen men, the count himself killed his rival.

The fifteenth-century château remains splendid, its chimneys, turrets and blue slate roofs reflected in the waters of the river. The memory of the ferocious sixteenth-century assassination does not spoil the deep peace of the village. The surrounding hills are planted with vines, and walks through the narrows village streets will lead through the vineyards to

two ancient windmills: Le Moulin de la Tranchée and, a little further on, the fully restored fifteenth-century Moulin de Hépinière.

Apart from the ruins of two twelfth-century churches, the other interest of the village lies in the remnants of hundreds of original troglodyte houses arranged in terraces and connected by a honeycomb of narrow paths. Some are crumbling but others are used for growing mushrooms or to age the wine of the illustrious neighbouring *domaines*. They provide perfect conditions for the successful storage of the wine: the caves are dark and the temperature is constant, with just the right degree of humidity. The extensive caves of Montsoreau have been used for this purpose since 1864, and today visitors can stop for a little *dégustation* of the best known, such as Saumur, Souzay-Champigny and Turquant. Just outside Montsoreau, on the way to Turquant, there is a complete troglodyte *auberge* where the wine is exceptional and the food classically French.

The most beautiful view in the Touraine is at Candes-Saint-Martin, where the river Loire joins the Vienne. To appreciate the splendour of the scene, climb the slope behind the church, admiring on the way the charm of the village's hidden corners.

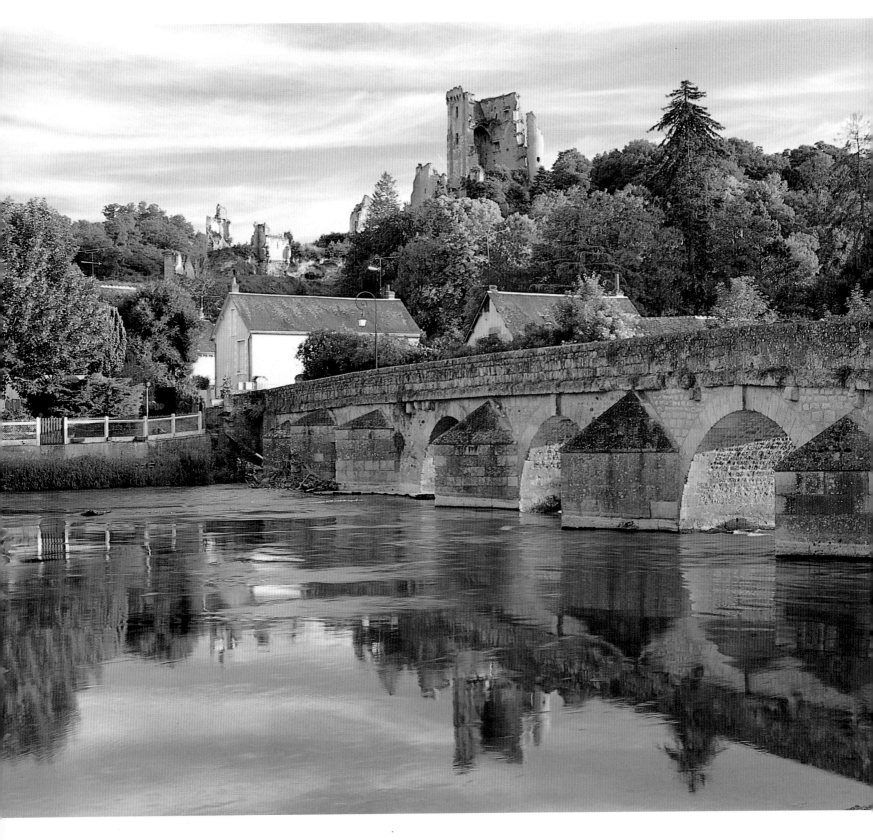

North of the Loire, one of its tributaries, confusingly called the Loir, runs through the lush, sensuous country of the Vendôme. Pierre Ronsard, the lyric poet who, like no other, sang the praises of women, was born at the Manoir de la Possonnière and not far away lies the Manoir de Bonaventure, family home of French romantic, Alfred de Musset. In between these two sources of romance, near the troglodyte villages of Trôo and Les Roches-l'Evêque, there is a village which holds all the magic of the Loire valley: Lavardin.

On the cliff overlooking the Loir, the ruins of a large feudal fortress hold their jagged silhouette against the sky. Beneath, among rose gardens and charming corners planted with ferns and medicinal herbs, the village is so perfect, so peaceful, that you need to slow down your pace to that of the meandering river.

Step on to the bridge which spans the river, close your eyes and all the sweet words of Ronsard, the poet who expressed with lyric perfection all the passion and transience of love, are conjured up:

> *Mignonne, allons voir si la rose*
> My dear, let us see if the rose
> *Qui avait ce matin déclose*
> Which only this morning unfurled
> *Sa robe de pourpre au soleil*
> Her robe of purple to the sun
> *N'a point perdu son pareil...*
> Has yet lost none of her beauty...

Then amble through sinuous medieval lanes to the Grande Rue, where half-timbering mixes harmoniously with mullions and turrets of tufa, the local porous stone. The church holds some of the best twelfth-century frescoes of the Loir valley.

At the *auberge*, as you savour a chilled Montlouis or a Vouvray *champagnisé*, ponder over the beauty of Lavardin's once-impenetrable fortress which saw the defeat of Richard the

Lionheart by the Comte de Vendôme in 1188.

South of Tours, the historic area of the Touraine opens up, watered by the Indre, the Indrois and the Cher. At the foot of a buttress of cliff, the long walled gardens of Montrésor slope down to the Indrois. Within its amphitheatre shape, medieval houses stand higgledy-piggledy among traditional *potagers*, where flowers and vegetables flourish in each other's company. Here and there, baskets in hand, the villagers making their way towards the few old-fashioned shops might be characters out of the minutely observed world of Honoré de Balzac, who described his native Touraine with such passion. Curiously, several of the old-world streets bear Polish names, for the elegant turreted château was bought by Count Branicki in the nineteenth century and is still owned by his family.

Despite this strange idiosyncrasy, Montrésor has escaped all form of restoration. The lower part of the village is reached across what used to be a drawbridge, and a walk past the old wash house, *lavoir*, and the fountain, brings you

Lavardin, in its wooded setting beside the river Loir, is a traditional medieval village. Not far from the church of Saint-Genest, with its exquisite twelfth- and sixteenth-century murals, is the old lavoir, *wash-house (above), now a restful place to watch the river go by.*

Lavardin's fort (opposite), set high on a rock, is now in ruins, but the ancient bridge has survived the attacks of two English kings: Henry II and Richard the Lionheart.

Cave cottages, such as this one in Montsoreau, are often refined into comfortable homes. Early troglodytes started to excavate the soft limestone of the Loire valley in the eleventh century, and in the nineteenth century, half the local population lived in these unconventional homes.

to fine examples of fourteenth- and fifteenth-century houses. A covered market survives from the seventeenth century as does, most remarkably, the old wool exchange, built on oak pillars with a patterned roof of slate and tiles. An ornate gateway opens on to a path up to rue Potocki which leads up to the château. From here there are magnificent views over the ancient rooftops: Montrésor is a village where time stands still.

Venturing further south will find you almost on the edge of the Berry. Slate has given way to tile, and limestone to granite, and the rich green landscape is reminiscent of the bucolic countryside described in the rustic novels of Amandine Aurore Lucile Dupin, better known to the world as George Sand. The spirited nineteenth-century novelist had a house at Gargilesse-Dampierre, described in *Promenades autour d'un village*, and revelled in exploring the area with such companions as Turgenev and Flaubert or her lovers Chopin and Liszt. Her house is now a small museum, her favourite possessions collected together here by her son Maurice, her grand-daughter Aurore, and many of her admirers.

Towering above the river Porte-feuille, Saint-Benoît-du-Sault is a lofty village built on a rocky bluff. The narrow houses cling together along the steep, winding lanes and ancient wrought-iron railings help the less agile make the climb to the top. Saint-Benoît welcomes each summer a splendid classical music festival.

The beauty of the village, clustered around the château and church, inspired not only George Sand but also Claude Monet, Théodore Rousseau and Henry James, who all settled in Gargilesse for a while. The softly painted shutters and doorways of brightly coloured summer flowers are still an artist's delight and in the narrow leafy lanes the mica-schist in the house walls glistens in the sun just like the river which flows alongside them.

The Loire valley and its tributaries such as the Cher or the Loir are a paradise for fresh-water fishing. As soon as the season opens, the green banks of the river Allier at Apremont-sur-Allier are lined with keen fishermen. Men of tradition who enjoy the rural pleasures of life, they shelter under huge umbrellas, silent and totally absorbed in their sport. Every species of river fish lives here, and the housewives of the region will teach you good local recipes such as *matelote d'anguille*, a dish of eel cooked in a rich wine sauce, or *brochet aux oignons* – pike cooked in white wine with onions, as well as carp in red wine.

Lying in one of the many luscious valleys on the western limit of the Burgundian hills,

At Gargilesse-Dampierre, beside the river Indre, French writers and artists would meet to effuse over the trees, the stone and water, misty mornings and distant church bells in their shared enjoyment of the Berrichon surroundings. Trees carefully trained over a garden path (opposite) sum up the idealized naturalness that appealed to the Romantics.

Apremont-sur-Allier is a medieval river village of honey-coloured stone and warm red roofs. Its ancient stone houses present an image of peace and pleasure, with numerous square turrets, outside staircases and carved balustrades. In the summer, when the river is at its lowest, fine beaches are exposed, and families come to bathe and picnic, a sight which, even today, recalls the colourful riverside gatherings so often depicted by French artists.

Apremont's sturdy and elegant château was first a feudal fortress which fell into a sad state of disrepair. In the eighteenth century, it was largely rebuilt and is still inhabited. When open it is well worth a visit, especially to the fine stables and coach house.

A more recent addition to Apremont's attractions is the stunning public garden, with bridges, gazebos and lush plantings all in the *style anglais*. Created as recently as the 1970s, the Parc Floral is a wonderful complement to Apremont's gentle and carefully preserved medieval beauty.

Pretty rows of cottages and willows lining the sleepy waters of the Allier conjure up the peace of Apremont-sur-Allier. Apremont's massive château (above), *with its immense expanse of roofs and turrets, provides a backdrop to the village.*

POITOU-CHARENTES

Poitou-Charentes is a huge rural area of marshland, vineyards and sunflower fields, with a sunny coastline where the sea pink grows wild and pine tree-clad dunes face the salty surf of the Atlantic ocean. But it is also an area with a colourful past and a remarkable heritage.

The ports of La Rochelle and Rochefort both illustrate the maritime vocation of the area, souvenirs of far-away conquests of the New World and the spicy Orient, and reminders of fierce battles in the shape of handsome fortifications. Samuel de Champlain, who founded Quebec, was born further down the coast at Brouage, whose fortress appears like a mirage at the centre of reclaimed marshes, a paradise for sea birds on the edge of the treasured oysterbeds of Marennes. Then, further south, at the edge of the Gironde estuary, stands Talmont, its large fishing nets set at the end of piers and a church which seems to have fallen from heaven, the purest example of religious architecture in this part of western France.

During the eleventh and twelfth centuries, over half a million pilgrims a year from northern France, Normandy, England and Ireland crossed the Poitou and the Saintonge on their way to Compostela, to worship Saint James (Santiago), the patron saint of northern Spain. These *coquillards*, as they were called, all bore the scallop-shell emblem of Saint James, hence today's French name of the scallop: *coquille Saint-Jacques*. Along the pilgrim route, sculpture and architecture flourished during this period from Poitiers to Talmont via Celles-sur-Belle, Melle, Angoulême and Saintes, capital of the Saintonge region and already a major centre in Roman times.

Of course we must not forget Cognac, a handsome historic town devoted to France's most civilized eau-de-vie. Grande champagne, fine champagne, petite champagne, borderies, fins bois, bons bois…all are different qualities of this double distillation of local white wine left to age in oak casks made by coopers in the Limousin. It was by mixing cognac with grape juice that Pineau des Charentes, an aperitif similar in taste to sherry, was invented in the sixteenth century.

Oysters, cognac, pineau, but also eels, sweet soles, mussels and a collection of little-known cheeses bearing the names of saints: Saint-Gelais, Saint-Loup, Saint-Maixent, and a butter, *beurre d'Echiré*, so fine it finds its way to the tables of Maxim's in Paris!…one would almost end up neglecting art and history, churches and villages to indulge in gourmandizing…

Lying off La Rochelle, the Ile de Ré has sandy beaches, whitewashed houses with green shutters and pink-tiled roofs, and, in summer, a riot of multicoloured hollyhocks. Here, life has revolved around wine and sea salt since the Middle Ages, when Cistercian monks from the

(page 48) *Overlooked by the isolated abbey of Talmont, many of the Gironde estuary's curious fishing huts on stilts are found here. Large fishing nets are hung from the front end and lowered into the sea at high tide.*

Pleasure boats at Ars-en-Ré (right), one of the Ile de Ré's ports. The thin, pointed steeple in the background belongs to the church of Saint-Etienne and was painted black and white to act as a landmark to guide boats into the harbour.

Vendée across the water started to contribute to the economy of the island by planting vines, exploiting the salt marshes and teaching the inhabitants to plough and farm. Their ruined abbey, Abbaye des Châteliers, can be seen near the village of La Flotte. It was, at the time, the largest Cistercian abbey in France.

Ré, Rey, Roy – the spelling varied through history – was a strategic place on the western coast of France. Once a Roman settlement (a Roman temple dedicated to Neptune was built there in 27BC), the island was invaded many times, and possession of the island was for four hundred years constantly a source of contention between the British and the French crowns. The large star-shaped fort at Saint-Martin, the village which is now the capital of the island, was built by Vauban, Louis XIV's great military engineer, to protect French interests.

The women of Ré may have forsaken the *quichenotte*, the traditional headdress, for a knotted scarf and the donkeys no longer wear stripy pantaloons (an unexplained idiosyncrasy of Ré until the last century), but the sheltered port still bustles with fishermen and fishing boats, as yachtsmen, housewives and restaurant owners come and buy the catch of the day direct from the boats. The quays are the ideal setting in which to sample the regional speciality, *mouclade*: mussels in their half-shells baked in a creamy sauce perfumed with Pineau Blanc. Perfect with a dry white Bordeaux.

The Ile de Ré is now tied to the mainland by a bridge and from springtime until the end of the summer, millions of visitors assault the sun-drenched beaches and maritime pine groves. But, out of season, the sunny island has managed to keep its misty charm. Blessed by a balmy micro-climate and exceptionally high rate of sunshine, every season bears its fruit, from the *fruits de mer* to grapes, and life for the inhabitants revolves not only around the sea, but also market gardening and wine.

Harvesting salt has been a tradition on the Ile de Ré for centuries. When the tide is at its highest, lock gates at the edge of the salt marshes are opened to replenish the basins, and the seawater is channelled through to small evaporation pools known as oeillets. The salt is then gathered in with a long-handled rake called an ételle.

On the Ile de Ré (bottom left), people who have never heard of going to a fishmonger buy fish straight from the boat on the quayside at La Flotte-en-Ré. Housewives (centre left) visiting the busy little market exchange the news of the day while choosing Charentais melons or oysters from the neighbouring oyster beds.

At the end of the nineteenth century, Ré was the last wine-growing area of south-west France to be affected by phylloxera. The vine louse which devastated the grapevines of the Bordeaux vineyards could not survive on the sand of the island, and the imposing houses which are to be seen in the villages of Sainte-Marie and Bois reflect the fortunes made by some island wine-growers in this black period for viniculture.

In the Baie du Fiers, on the western edge of the island, the land gained from the sea has an exceptionally sunny position and is blessed with favourable winds, a propitious climate for the extraction of sea salt. The exploitation of the salt marshes dates back about nine centuries, to the time of those enterprising monks from the Vendée. Trade in salt thrived until the beginning of the nineteenth century, at which time up to 30,000 tonnes found their way to Newfoundland and brown-sailed barges from Scandinavia called at the port of Le Fier on their way to the New World. The island later found itself competing with salt from Portugal and the

At the end of a garden path in Arcais (opposite), *two flat-bottomed punts await their owners, who will paddle through the watery maze of the Marais Poitevin to church or to transport their cattle to outlying pastures.*

Mediterranean, and since the Second World War trade has dwindled.

Many abandoned marshes have become a paradise for ornithologists, as colonies of birds stop on their long trip through Europe to rest on the island. What is left of the salt marshes is still worked with techniques unchanged through the centuries, and from May to September, as the sun's sinking rays turn the embedded salt to the colour of amethyst, the salt farmer can be seen still gently raking away. The salt fields are cut into small squares surrounded by clay walks; in the beds, the water is left until it evaporates, leaving behind the crystallized salt.

Overlooking the salt marshes, the village of Ars-en-Ré has the characteristic charm of island dwellings. Flower-clad whitewashed houses line narrow streets, and the high-walled courtyards set in between give a Moorish appearance to the place. Fig trees, mimosa and sun-gorged vines complete the southern feel. In contrast is the steeple of the village church. Not only is it crooked since it was hit by lightning in 1840, but it is painted a startling black and white – unusual, but practical as it serves as a land-mark for sailors who use the channel from the Bucheron sandbank.

On the mainland, water continues to fashion the landscape. Known as the Venise Verte, 'green Venice', the Marais Poitevin is a unique maze of fens, dykes and slow-flowing rivers separated by small fields and luscious greenery, a silent and peaceful oasis, where even for the farmer, life is spent at the pace of a gliding punt.

In summer, thick foliage hangs over the waterways and the banks are filled with irises, wild mint, meadowsweet and angelica. The whole area is a paradise for the toad and the coypu, the heron and the kingfisher. And while the dragonfly busies itself over the water surface, eel, gudgeon, carp and tench hide under the leafy water lentil. Simple homes and villages have grown up at the water's edge.

A typical house near Coulon, the main village of the Marais Poitevin. Known as Venise Verte, 'green Venice', the Marais is a complex network of backwaters with an extremely rich flora and fauna.

Not far from Poitiers, once held by the Black Prince, is the riverside village of Angles-sur-l'Anglin (above and centre). It is reputed that its name derives from 'England', and to this day the inhabitants of Angles are called les Anglais. The old school rooms house a school of embroidery which has been passing the skill down to the young girls of five successive generations.

Exploring the village of Coulon and wandering through the hamlet of Arcais will reveal the archetypal *maisons des marais*: low, whitewashed houses with attics closed with latticed wood and round-tiled roofs. They festoon the water's edge with geranium-clad windows and brightly painted shutters. Along the grassy banks, fishermen sit under large umbrellas to tease the freshwater fish. The restaurants serve simple local food, such as frogs' legs, or a scrumptious dish of eel fried with thick slices of potatoes and served with garlic butter. But the older women have more secret recipes and if you are lucky one may even reveal the art of preparing a sweet liquor of angelica. The same woman will probably watch visitors on the punts and, with a tear in her eyes and a nostalgic smile on her face recall the days of *maraichinage*, when courting couples were allowed to make secret assignations on the fens,

exchanging their love and kisses under the privacy of the punt's huge black umbrella.

Further east, the land is drier, but water does not lose its hold. Huddled between Poitou and the hills of the Berry, Angles-sur-l'Anglin is a magnet for fishermen. Built on the banks of the river Anglin, Angles has a riverside footpath which runs alongside houses made pretty with pale shutters and sweet-smelling climbing plants. Walled terraced gardens are covered with vines and huge aquamarine dragonflies balance on the leaves of waterlilies in the slow-moving river. An old watermill, complete with wheel, faces the chapel across the river which was once part of a medieval abbey. The lower village, the *ville basse*, is dominated by the castle and the walk up the steep hill to the *ville haute* is past the studded doors of medieval houses standing cheek-by-jowl with large nineteenth-century *maisons de maître*.

Villebois-Lavalette, perched on an escarpment south of Angoulême, has a long military history. Once an ancient Gaulish settlement, it has had two later fortresses. One, in the eleventh century, is now in ruins but its seventeenth-century successor still stands, and looking out over the distant views over the surrounding plateaux, it is obvious that Villebois was the ideal spot for strategic defence.

The countryside around Villebois is rich and so the market held every Saturday morning inside the seventeenth-century *halles* is a cornucopia of delights: honey, local cheeses such as creamy caillebotte and sharp goat's milk cheeses, liver pâté flavoured with cognac, and all the fresh seasonal vegetables from the surrounding market-gardens. Spring brings tiny sweet peas and beans and delectable asparagus, while with the summer months comes the rich aroma of the sun-gorged Charentais melon.

A few kilometres away, Aubeterre-sur-Dronne is tucked away between the Angoumois and the Périgord in a region where you feel you have

The waters of the Anglin are a fisherman's paradise. The castle at Angles, forming the backdrop to a peaceful fishing scene in an old mill pool, witnessed fierce battles during the Hundred Years War.

At Villebois-Lavalette, near Angoulême, the capital of the Saintonge, weekly markets are held under the magnificent seventeenth-century halle (left), cleverly built to follow the slope of the square.

reached the south. The village, carved out of the calcareous cliffs of the Dronne, has cascades of bright flowers pouring out of ancient wood loggias, brown-tiled roofs, palm trees and sinuous stepped alleyways. By lunchtime the unmistakable smell of fresh garlic hangs out of the balconies – this could be Spain. The tall houses have been built on terraces all the way up to the huge fourteenth-century château, which is itself surrounded by an unusual covered balcony. Underneath lies the curiosity of the village: a subterranean church which dates from the eleventh century. It is a rare example of monolithic excavation. The disciples of Saint Maur carved this church out of a single piece of rock, to accommodate relics from the Crusades. The nave is over 20 m long and the

baptistery, which was used for total immersion, was fed with water springing from the cliff. Nowadays, villagers worship in the église Saint-Jacques, whose name and Spanish-style geometrical portal are reminders that Aubeterre was on the pilgrim route to Santiago de Compostela – several of the solid houses along rue Saint-Jacques were once convents. Also along here is the ropemaker's house, with an elaborate Renaissance façade. There was a time when Aubeterre was linked with the maritime activities of the coast, hemp grew in the region and ropes and thick cloth were among the industrial activities which provided the village with a livelihood. Today it is still a lively village, one of many in France which makes one think: if only I could live here.

Aubeterre-sur-Dronne (right) gets its name from Alba Terra, after the white limestone cliffs into which it nestles. Its situation, which put it in the path of invading Moors and on the pilgrim route to Santiago de Compostela, has contributed to its surprisingly Spanish look.

MASSIF CENTRAL

The Massif Central, at the heart of France, is a large nature reserve, peaceful, mysterious and old-fashioned, where country women still make lace on the doorsteps of the villages.

Set at the crossroads of four provinces, it spreads from the pasturelands of the Haut-Limousin, south to the Causses of the Quercy and from the forests of the Périgord Vert to its east to the volcanic mountains of the Auvergne in the west. Among wooded valleys and solitary lakes, the moorlands are covered with heather and gorse, the saffron crocus grows with the yellow gentian and the wild mushroom under the chestnut tree. On the volcanic grounds of the Haute-Loire, the spring slopes are blue with the delicate flower of that most sought-after lentil, the green *lentille du Puy*. Water springs everywhere, even in the craters of the volcanoes, and names like Vichy, Volvic and Perrier are associated with good health and mineral water.

The region is associated with industry, but much of it predates Monsieur Michelin and the tyre factory he established in Clermont-Ferrand in 1830. In the vale of Larga, paper is still hand-made, a few tapestry workshops survive at Aubusson, the French countryman's knife, the *opinel*, is made at Thiers and, of course, Limoges is synonymous with the finest of porcelain.

Tenacious and diverse, the villages are solidly built with the raw material from the area. Whether it is granite, *lauze* or lava, the quarries of the Massif have paved streets, built fort-resses and cathedrals throughout France. In the north of the region stone houses are tiled with schist, while in the south the tiles are red with terracotta. From Lavaudieu to Aurillac, the rivers are often bordered by houses with wooden balconies. Enormous bread ovens, *lavoirs* (wash houses) and mills are still in use in the smaller villages.

The people of central France are solid, welcoming and happy. It is one of the last regions of France where the local dances and music have survived. And it is never a surprise, after a solid meal of *bréjaude*, a hearty soup, and a stuffed-cabbage *farcidure*, to see people dancing to the sound of the accordion and the *cornemuse*.

In the autumn the forest of Tronçais, north of Montluçon, is majestic when the leaves of the largest oak plantation in Europe are turning to gold. This is the forest that supplies Cognac with its oak barrels, and some specimens are three hundred years old. The wild boar, stag, hare and rabbit have found their home in the thickets, and long avenues through the wood-land lead to small villages and isolated ponds. A restaurant hidden away at the centre specializes in fine game dishes in season. At the southern tip of the forest, a road follows the valley of the

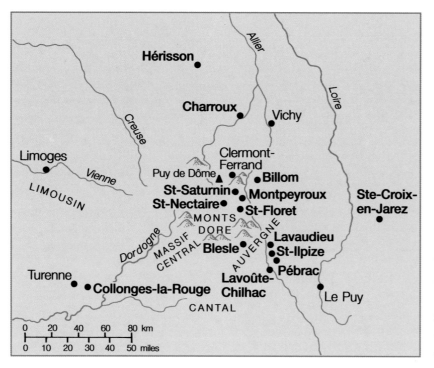

Hérisson

Charroux Vichy

Clermont-
Ferrand
Puy de Dôme Billom
St-Saturnin Montpeyroux Ste-Croix-
St-Nectaire St-Floret en-Jarez
MONTS
DORE
Lavaudieu
Blesle St-Ilpize
Pébrac
Lavoûte-
Chilhac Le Puy
CANTAL

Limoges
Allier
Creuse
Loire
Vienne
LIMOUSIN
Dordogne
MASSIF CENTRAL
AUVERGNE

Turenne
Collonges-la-Rouge

0 20 40 60 80 km
0 10 20 30 40 50 miles

(page 60) The village of Hérisson, overlooking the river Aumance, has kept the bucolic atmosphere depicted by landscape artist Henri Harpignies. He painted many corners of this medieval village, capturing the distinctive aspect of its houses, with their side-steps and railings leading to the front door.

river Aumance past two handsome châteaux, Le Creux and La Roche. Suddenly, the impressive silhouette of the towers of Hérisson stands out, on the tip of a huge rock overhanging a meander of the river. The spot had been judiciously chosen by the Sire de Bourbon as a strategic military observatory, and a small fort was first erected in the eleventh century. A large fortress succeeded in the thirteenth century, which was then extended into a large château.

Hérisson has no ramparts left but two gateways leading into the village remain. The houses are tightly packed in convoluted lanes between the church and château; most of them were built in the seventeenth century with stones from the old castle. Walking up through the wooded hill behind the village, the view down is of the intricate pattern of heather-coloured, high-pitched roofs interspersed with the spires of poplars that border the river. The scene cannot fail to seduce an artist, and in the mid-nineteenth century Henri Harpignies, a landscape artist who belonged to the Ecole de

Barbizon with contemporaries such as Corot and Rousseau, immortalized every facet of Hérisson on canvas. His best painting is of the Saut-du-Loup, Wolf's Leap, a bucolic cascade down-stream from the village.

One of the natural riches of the Massif Central has been used for centuries to pave the streets of France: the blue or beige granite extracted in the quarries of the Auvergne.

The stonework of Charroux tells the history of the place. Once a bastion of the Bourbon family, this was a home of the rich, where elegance prevailed. Charroux is a sturdy testimony of the past and a rare example of the art of stone cutting and carving.

The main gateway is now a *pigeonnier*, and, ransacked by the Huguenots in the fifteenth century, only one half-timbered house with corbelling remains. But the whole village has, none the less, retained much evidence of the substantial life people must have led here. The streets are paved, and the façades of the houses display fine ornamental stonework and heavy mullioned windows, such as the house in rue de la Poulaillerie, which was home to the Prince de Condé. One after the other, from *maisons bourgeoises* to aristocratic abodes, the houses tell the story of the village until the middle of the eighteenth century.

Even the local culinary speciality makes use of stone. Charroux's fine mustard, believed to have been created by the monks of the old abbey, is made by crushing the seeds with an old stone mill; the renowned wine of Saint-Pourçain is added to create a paste which is strong but not bitter, and full of aroma.

The immediate countryside is pretty, with sloping orchards and gardens running down towards the river Sioude. The imposing farm-houses were once part of the old city. All around there are distant views towards the Montagne Bourbonnaise, the Massif Central and the Forêt des Colettes planted in the seventeenth century.

On the eastern slopes of the Massif, the road from the Rhône valley winds past banks planted with vines and fruit trees to reach the small valley of the river Couzon. In a detour along a sunken lane is the entrance gate of an old charterhouse. When the Carthusian monks built Sainte-Croix-en-Jarez, little did they know that, after the French Revolution, the farmers and artisans of the region would buy the whole monastery to turn it into the unusual village that it is today.

The village has no street, only two large courtyards linked by a long vaulted passageway.

A few rooms of the old priory – the old kitchen, the library and the abbot's room – have been turned into a museum. But the official structure of a French village is all there: the church, the *mairie*, a restaurant, and village houses with little gardens, once cultivated by monks. Life here still seems to be spent in almost monkish self-sufficiency.

Seen from the gardens of its château, the circular medieval village of Saint-Saturnin on the edge of France's volcanic heartland, looks like the perfect setting for a play: red-roofed houses surround the square, a fountain at its

Charroux is a village famous for its stone quarries. Throughout the village are examples of the work of local stonemasons, from handsome doorways to small paved court-yards and the amazingly narrow pavements.

centre, soft hills rise to opalescent skies in the background. Is Monsieur le Curé about to burst into song as he leaves the church? Well, if he was, it would not be comic opera but drama, for it was here that the tragic story of Marguerite de Valois, la Reine Margot, was played out. The de La Tour d'Auvergne family, had owned the château and village since the thirteenth century, and the young queen was to be the last Dame de Saint-Saturnin. But she was imprisoned here by her Machiavellian mother, Catherine de' Medici, at the time of her wedding to Henri de Navarre and the massacre of the Huguenots on St Bartholemew's Eve. The sad fate of the young queen, as recounted by Alexandre Dumas in *La Reine Margot*, is a favourite French classic.

Inside the church, the coat of arms of Henri IV and Marguerite de Valois is set in gold in the altarpiece of the choir, and there is an alleyway of trees dedicated to her. Each summer, large marguerites bloom in the fountain outside the château... Saint-Saturnin still weeps for her young queen. But Saint-Saturnians must have a very philosophical approach to life, for above the entrance of the old cemetery is inscribed: 'We have been like you. One day, you will be like us. Think about it.'

On the south-eastern tip of the Auvergne, near Saint-Etienne, the ancient charterhouse of Sainte-Croix-en-Jarez (opposite) is now a hamlet where a life of self-sufficiency is spent in ecclesiastical calm.

In the peace of the Auvergne, surrounded by the mountains of the Monts Dore, lies Saint-Saturnin. Its solidly built Romanesque church is charged with tales of horror of France's most Machiavellian queen, Catherine de' Medici.

Inside Saint-Floret's castle (right and centre), *the ribs of lofty vaulting meet at a rose carved with a smiling angel.*

From the volcanic mountains of the Monts Dore to the town of Issoire, which boasts one of the most interesting churches in the Auvergne, there is a fascinating drive to take along the course of the Couze Pavin. A *couze* is a torrent which follows the route of a lava flow, where water gushes along the trench formed by the incandescent molten rock which often found its way through deep, narrow gorges.

A *couze* always springs from a volcanic lake. The black waters of Lac Pavin are found some 1197 m up and fill to a depth of 92 m the immense crater of a volcano. The site is completely protected from the wind by the crater's encircling cliffs and, at all times the surface of the water remains still and limpid. The sight chills the spine, so it is not surprising to hear that the name of the lake originates from the Latin *pavens*, which means 'terrifying'.

After the village of Cheix, the road passes upright columns of basalt, ancient troglodyte houses and a tenth-century chapel with frescoes. At Cotteuse the road crosses the Couze which

then runs into a narrow gorge towards Saint-Floret. Built among granite rocks, the village is dominated by a thirteenth-century fortress built high on a rock. In the donjon is a Gothic room with a vaulted ceiling crowned by an intricate stone rose. On the walls some fine murals depict a tale of chivalry. The Pont de la Pède has crossed the Couze in the centre of the village since the sixteenth century; on it is a tiny oratory with, inside, a charming statue of the Virgin Mary. From the low road a path takes you to the butte du Chastel and its Romanesque church, with a remarkable fifteenth-century mural representing Jean de Bellenaves, Seigneur of Saint-Floret, being introduced by John the Baptist to the Madonna and Child.

A natural hot-water spa town founded by the Romans, Saint-Nectaire nestles on the slopes of the volcanic Mont Cornadore. From the top of

The tiny village of Saint-Floret is half-hidden among the volcanic rocks and torrents of the Couze Pavin. A picturesque route follows the treacherous beds left by lava flows from a lake that was once an immense volcanic crater, down to the fields and vineyards of the Limagne.

The Auvergne, land of extinct volcanoes, is a maze of streams and natural springs – most of France's mineral waters originate from here. As well as spa water rich in medicinal benefits, Saint-Nectaire (above) offers prime examples of rural architecture. Within the plain lines of its Romanesque church are hidden treasures.

the hill are commanding views over France's most picturesque volcanic chain, a landscape which is pure tranquillity broken only by the fluttering of a bright butterfly, or the quick shriek of a sparrowhawk.

The old village of Saint-Nectaire-le-Haut is overlooked by a magnificent church of the purest architecture, an expression of the finest Romanesque art. Its treasure is a reliquary of Saint Baudine in enamelled copper. The art of enamelling started in the Middle Ages in the nearby Limousin, and most of the enamelled copper treasures found in French churches were made in Limoges. The first workshops were started in Limoges in the tenth century by Venetian artists. The enamel is made from a leaded glass base coloured, by fusion, with oxides of gold, silver, cobalt, manganese and uranite found in the subsoil of the region. It is now a rare commodity.

Another local rarity is, sadly, a farm-made Saint-Nectaire cheese, left to mature inside thin wooden round cases called *fourmes*. (It is this *fourme*, the local patois for *forme* (shape), which gave the French the name for cheese, for the process was called *formage*, which then became *fromage*.)

There are three main cheeses from the Auvergne: fourme d'Ambert, a very creamy blue-veined cheese, Cantal and Saint-Nectaire. All three are made with the milk of the numerous cows that graze the pastures of the volcanic slopes. Today, they are all standardized and made in large regulated dairies with heavily pasteurized milk. Gone are the days when one

Among the bustle of the Saturday market in Le Puy can be found stalls selling seasonal fruit, local farm cheeses, choice charcuterie and, in season, many fascinating types of wild mushroom gathered from the surrounding fields and the magnificent forest of La Chaise-Dieu.

Wild flowers grow in great profusion and variety among the cultivated orchards in the pure air of the Auvergne. This spring landscape (centre) is near Saint-Saturnin.

could go directly to the farm to buy a Saint-Nectaire, with its distinctive grey rind marbled by yellow and red lichen. They were sold in threes, tied with a piece of straw. Saint-Nectaire has never been a cheap cheese, but when you know that it takes 15 litres of milk to make a cheese which weighs 1.5 kg and contains 65 per cent fat you will understand why. Some traditional cheese farms still exist, but for how much longer?

South of the Auvergne, along the wild, unpredictable torrent of the river Allier, lies the paradise of the Haute-Loire. This is lace country. The museum at Blesle has over 300 lace bonnets and *coiffes* on display, but the Route de la Dentelle really starts at Brioude, and the medieval city is well worth a stop if only to visit the exceptional lace museum, which describes the fine art of the region.

From Brioude the Route runs all the way to Le Puy, French capital city of lace, but in Lavaudieu you can still see lace-makers at work. Most women of the region have been taught from youth by their mothers and grandmothers and, in the summer, it is a common sight to find women sitting in the sunlit doorways of their houses, a lace cushion on their lap. It is a joy to watch these *dentellières*, tying the fine thread from pin to pin with such dexterity.

Lavaudieu is built along the lower valley of the river Sénouire, well protected from the excesses of the winter climate. All is tranquil here, and as you walk along the water meadows to admire the wooden balconies of the stone houses, all you can hear is the murmur of the

The small monastery of Lavaudieu was built in the eleventh century by Saint Robert, founder of the large abbey of La Chaise-Dieu. Restored by a master sculptor, the Corinthian columns of the cloister create an overwhelming sense of peace and tranquillity.

A shaded walk in Montpeyroux, not in cloisters, but under the vaults created by the Auvergne's accomplished masons. The region's stone is evident in the paved lanes, cobbled walls and the handsomely cut arches and doorways.

river. No wonder the Benedictine monks chose
to settle there in 1057. They built an abbey with
the only preserved cloister in the Auvergne,
impeccably restored by master sculptor Philippe
Kaeppelin. As if to match the wooden balconies
of the surrounding medieval village, a wooden
gallery runs around the first floor of the
cloister's quadrangle, supported by fluted
double Corinthian pillars. Inside the church,
there is a remarkable ensemble of wall paintings
of the fourteenth-century Italian school, with a
very striking allegory of the Black Death. The

twelfth-century frescoes of the refectory are
of Byzantine influence. The vineyards of
Lavaudieu have disappeared but the *maisons
vigneronnes* are still here, along the tortuous
lanes that lead to the village square, and rural
life and crafts are well presented in the Maison
des Arts Populaires.

South of Brioude and Lavaudieu, the road
follows the romantic meanders of the river
Allier. On early autumn mornings a soft mist
hangs over the valley, dripping crystalline beads
through the craze of large cobwebs strung

*In the village of Lavoûte-Chilhac,
near Lavaudieu, the river Allier
has almost dried up, leaving
exposed the complete infra-
structure of the terraced houses
that line the river. The extra-deep
bases are needed to cope with the
torrent the river becomes in winter.*

through the blades of grass. It is as if, since twilight, Nature had tried to compete with all the *dentellières* of the region.

At a bend of the river, the tiny fortified village of Saint-Ilpize suddenly appears. Set on a black basalt rock, the village huddles inside the curtain wall of its ramparts. If the château is in ruins, the black earth retains the heat, and exotic plants bloom in the gardens. The village's fourteenth-century chapel is extremely unusual with bells set in the basalt side wall and an apse of multi-coloured volcanic tufa.

Immediately across the valley, Villeneuve d'Allier seems ready to retaliate from the attacks of the ruined castle. And downstream, there is Lavoûte-Polignac with its fairytale sixteenth-century château, then Pébrac where the church retains another amazing enamelled brass casket and a unique polychromatic Nativity scene. From here to the west and the rubicund splendours of Collonges-la-Rouge, and all the way down to the Dordogne, you meet a string of villages whose names finish in 'ac', and

Lavaudieu, beside the Sénouire (above), *has a museum devoted to life and traditions in the Haute-Loire. It would be a mistake to describe this life as bygone, for women here still make fine Le Puy lace as displayed in the museum, and some people continue to speak the strange local patois heavily larded with Arabic words left behind by the Moors.*

So typical of the Haute-Loire, Saint-Ilpize (left) *is built on a rock of black lava. Fields around are devoted to the cultivation of green lentils, a speciality of the region that flourishes on the immensely fertile volcanic soil.*

In the sixteenth and seventeenth centuries, the local aristocracy of Collonges-la-Rouge (opposite) built opulent homes with myriad towers and turrets. This striking architecture is emphasized by the rich colour of the local stone, which gave the village its name.

you then realize that you have crossed the linguistic frontier. In the Gaulish terminology of the south, 'ac', being short for 'acus', designated a Gallo-Roman villa.

On a late summer's afternoon, the whole village of Collonges-la-Rouge stands incandescent and glowing against the wild chestnut and walnut groves of the Limousin hills. Known as 'the village of twenty-five towers' it stands, solid, exceptionally beautiful, almost foreign, preserved from the medieval times when pilgrims paused here on their way to Compostela. André Maurois said of Collonges: 'One often spends a lifetime ignoring the surrounding wonders of this world. Collonges is a jewel which deserves that foreigners cross an ocean to see it.'

The ruby glow comes from the red granite

which, extracted from the nearby quarry of Meyssac, has not only been used for the walls but also, in fine layers, for the roofs. An ancient Roman settlement, Colonica started to expand in the eighth century when an abbey was built. The village prospered between the sixteenth and eighteenth centuries with the commerce of wine and walnut oil. It was in this era of prosperity that, to match the castles built for the viscounts of Turenne in the previous century, the bourgeoisie of Collonges erected patrician houses and mansions which are still today solidly part of the village.

Among them, the Castel de Maussac, is distinguished by a square tower and fine turret. Its Renaissance door is engraved with the scallop shell of the Santiago pilgrims. The Castel de Vassinhac, built in the fifteenth and

Billom (right), at the foot of the Livradois hills, was an important city in the Middle Ages – the Auvergne's first university was built here. Today, an important garlic market is held along its ancient streets.

sixteenth centuries by the seigneurs of Collonges is a curiously squat building with mullioned windows, flanked by a solid square tower on one side, a fine bartizan on the other side and, at the centre, another heavy square tower with an entrance door surrounded by a splendid architrave.

The most elegant building must be the Maison de la Sirène. The house is named after the ornate carving on the door, which represents a mermaid holding a mirror in one hand and a comb in the other. The church, with its twelfth-century Limousin-style bell tower, is an architectural splendour. The tympanum over the door, strikingly white against the rubiginous

architecture, was carved in the white sandstone of Turenne by sculptors of the Toulouse School, and depicts the Second Coming of Christ. It is outlined by a pointed arch ornamented with a fine border of carved animals. Near the church, through one of the surviving gateways of the outer wall, is the pillared grain hall, and, in a courtyard, the remains of the village bakehouse.

Collonges is on the doorstep of the Dordogne, famed for, among other delicacies, its ducks and geese, so it is perhaps fitting that here in Collonges there should be the Musée Vivant de l'Oie, which not only records in detail the history of the goose, but is home to dozens of different species.

Medieval Limousin flourished as never before or since. Several of its prominent churchmen became pope and its troubadours were acclaimed. Turenne (opposite), *home of the illustrious de Turenne family and an independent viscounty until 1738, evokes this golden age of the Limousin. It had a profound influence on the architecture of villages such as Collonges-la-Rouge* (below), *whose beauty was praised by author Jean Giraudoux.*

DORDOGNE AND QUERCY

Périgord, Quercy, Rouergue, Guyenne...the mere mention of the names of these ancient French provinces of the south-west evokes images of splendid dishes of goose, wild mushrooms, the rich wine of Cahors, potatoes richly glazed with goose fat. And truffles. No wonder so many people will never reach the promised south...

But food and good wine are not all the area has to offer. It is steeped in history and has been a favoured habitation of mankind for millennia. Schoolboys exploring a cave near Les Eyzies in the nineteenth century discovered traces of Cro-Magnon Man. In the vast limestone caves of Lascaux, Roufignac and elsewhere the tall, powerful hunters and warriors of the Palaeolithic era left the legacy of their astonishing rock paintings.

In historic time, the region fell foul of waves of invaders: the Gauls were subdued by the Romans, whose dominance was in turn ended by Visigoth and other barbarian hordes attacking from the north. The marriage of Henry Plantagenet to Eleanor of Aquitaine brought much of France under the crown of England and the ensuing Hundred Years War came to an end only in 1453. In the sixteenth century, thirty years of turbulence continued to tear the region

apart, as Catholic killed Protestant, and Huguenot warred against Papist in the Wars of Religion.

The architecture of the region reflects the long struggle through the centuries. Stronghold villages, known as *castelnaux*, dot the Dordogne, and at the end of the eleventh century new villages, *sauveterres*, were built on land around the abbeys to be worked by freed serfs. In this region of religious strife, the monuments to religion are awe-inspiring, from the splendour of Rocamadour and Conques to the great cathedral of Périgueux, purportedly a model for the Sacré-Coeur in Paris.

Périgueux's immaculate cathedral suggested the name Périgord Blanc, and in a landscape as varied as the cultural heritage, the other regions of the Périgord are also distinguished by colour: the Périgord Vert in the north has as its backdrop the westernmost hills of the Limousin; Périgord Violet is coloured by the rich wines of the Agenais and the Bergeracois, and finally the thick dark oakwoods around Sarlat have given Périgord Noir its name.

At the heart of the Périgord Noir, among groomed châteaux and prehistoric painted caves, Saint-Amand-de-Coly has a supreme example of a fortified Romanesque church. It

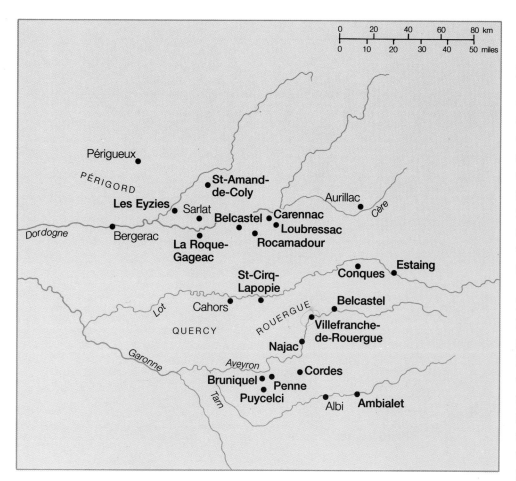

stands with great delicacy high above the grey *lauze* roofs of the village. Founded by an Augustinian canon in the twelfth century, it is a brilliant specimen of military architecture, its defences leaving nothing to chance. A moat runs all the way round and a passage once skirted the eaves, with numerous positions for archers' arrows and blind stairways to mislead the attackers. If you don't mind heights, one of the secret staircases will take you first to a gallery from which there is a magnificent view into the church and then to more stairs from the top of which the view over the surrounding countryside is breathtaking.

South, via the spectacular caves at Les Eyzies, and the pretty medieval city of Sarlat brings you close to the river Dordogne. In the morning, when the sun glows on the pale gold houses and ancient tiled roofs, the Dordogne valley village of La Roque-Gageac, could alone represent *la douceur de vivre* of this well-visited region of the south-west. The houses, clinging to the rock beside the river, reflect their splendid style in the calm waters below. The village has picturesque alleyways lined with artisans' houses and noble mansions such as the Château de la Malartrie, a splendid copy of fifteenth-century architecture. From the church built into the rock face there is a wonderful view of the meandering river.

(page 78) *At Loubressac the lush landscape follows the soft meanders of the Lot. Among its wooded hillsides stand romantic châteaux, ancient seigneurial houses and former hunting lodges.*

Hidden staircases and passageways will take the most daring visitor to the top of the fortifed church at Saint-Amand-de-Coly (left), near Sarlat. From the top the vista is extraordinary, looking out over the remains of the fortress, the village and the fertile landscape.

The château at Belcastel (opposite), on the river Dordogne, is on a marked walker's path which crosses the region, linking Souillac to Figeac, via Rocamadour.

At a time when the Dordogne was a commercial waterway, La Roque-Gageac was a favoured halt for the brown-sailed barges that plied the river. With its honey-coloured houses huddled against the cliff and its peaceful river frontage, the village remains one of the most striking villages along the Dordogne.

The region is a favourite centre for holidays, offering a lot of sightseeing but also a lot of gourmandizing. Delicious wine from the Bergeracois, foie gras, *confit* of goose, truffles cooked in the ash of the fireplace, eggs baked with freshly picked wild *cèpes* are all mouthwatering specialities. The region's climate has encouraged the planting of many orchards, and this is the largest centre in France for jams and preserves, especially an unforgettable, delicious chestnut jam.

Nearby is the idyllic village of Carennac whose praises were sung by French theologian and author, François Fénelon. Fénelon wrote his masterpiece, *Les Aventures de Télémaque*, in the tower which is named after him in Carennac – for five years he was prior of the monastic house near the river. The entrance porch is a masterpiece of Romanesque sculpture of the same school as Moissac or Beaulieu-sur-Dordogne, and the peaceful cloisters have three Gothic flamboyant galleries, the fourth being Romanesque.

The village is a fine collection of typical Quercy houses, built of soft ochre-coloured sandstone and covered with mossy brown-tiled roofs. Ivy and vine clad the walls and many of the old wooden balconies are weighed down by a medley of flowers. The fine turrets of the fifteenth-century château complete this picturesque ensemble.

Placid and inviting, the Dordogne (opposite) *winds westward from the old* bastide *town of Domme, on its way to Bordeaux.*

Carennac (right) *occupies a privileged position on the Dordogne, opposite a romantic islet called Calypso. Sailing barges like the one moored behind the fifteenth-century priory were once a common sight along these waters.*

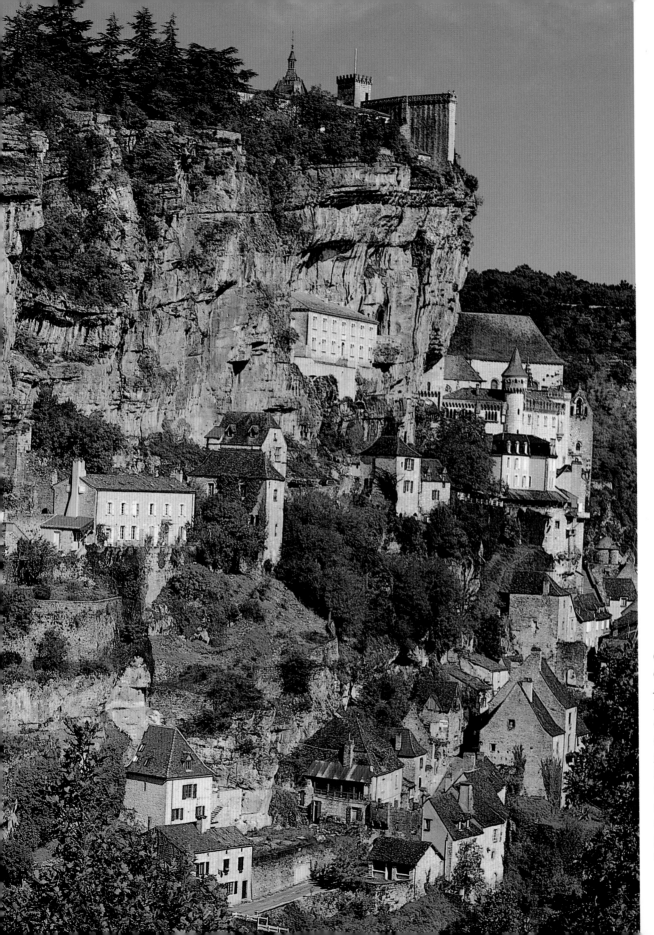

Clinging spectacularly to the sheer cliff over a gorge on the river Alzou, the medieval village of Rocamadour (left and opposite) is a major site of pilgrimage. In ancient times the pilgrims' penance was to climb on their knees up the 216 steps leading to the chapel of Notre Dame. From a distance Rocamadour, with its seven churches and vertiginously perched houses, appears to hang right over the gorge.

South of the Dordogne and Carennac the Quercy has kept its wild beauty. The vast plateau is cut by deep, magnificent gorges like the Causse de Gramat, which holds two exceptional sites: the gigantic limestone swallow-hole of Padirac, and Rocamadour.

It is midday, on 15 August, in the Quercy. The sound of an organ and a joyful hymn to the Virgin Mary, sung in Occitan dialect, reverberate around the vaults of the Basilique Saint-Sauveur in Rocamadour. This village and sanctuary, built by audacious monks in the Middle Ages, hangs, seemingly impossibly, over an abyss. Houses and seven chapels overlap each other, as if holding on to each other to maintain their balance. Seen from the cliff-top castle, this architectural bet with God and nature makes you reel.

The valley of the river Alzou which runs at the foot of Rocamadour was already a sacred site in prehistoric times. Later, early Christian anchorites lived in the grottoes and surrounding caves, and in 1166 the body of a hermit found buried under a small chapel dedicated to the Virgin Mary was canonized under the name of Saint Amadour ('lover of the rock' in Occitan). Miracles started to happen on the spot and soon Rocamadour became one of the most popular Christian pilgrimage centres. Ruined by religious wars and the French Revolution, it was revived as a place of devotion by the archbishops of Cahors in the last century. Today, coach after coach bring millions of devout pilgrims each year to the seven sanctuaries.

Clustered around the base of the double-naved basilica of Saint-Sauveur are the chapels and holy places which are the focus of religious attraction; among them the twelfth-century crypt of Saint-Amadour, the chapel of the Black Madonna, to whom the monks dedicated their endeavours, the Chapelle Saint-Michel, with medieval frescoes in azure and gold.

At the foot of these shrines, the picturesque

ancient village spreads along a steep hill which leads down to the shady water meadows of the valley below. The quartier de la Louve is a splendid mixture of medieval architecture with rounded soft walls in local stone, oval openings, timber work infilled with pale ochre daub. The shaded gardens are welcome arbours of greenery. But cross the river and it is only then, up the opposite hill that, framed by the wood of La Pannonie, can the truly breathtaking site of Rocamadour be appreciated.

Few places can exceed Rocamadour's dizzying cliff-face position, but rarely does a village and its natural surroundings merge so successfully as Saint-Cirq-Lapopie and the steep wooded slopes of the Lot.

Jewel of the Aquitaine, Saint-Cirq lost its fortress on the orders of Louis XI back in the fifteenth century, but has kept a timeless and well-protected architectural unity, where no modern addition has ever been allowed. Timber-framed houses with arched Gothic or mullioned windows illustrate the history of the village. Halfway up the hill comes the first glimpse of the peaceful green valley over an expanse of ancient clay-tiled roofs and manicured terraced gardens where roses, hollyhocks and honeysuckle flourish. A further climb reaches the Gothic church with, at one side, a small Romanesque chapel. On the way you will notice the unfamiliar names of the streets. They and others refer, in Occitan, to the trade of the artisans who lived and worked there: Pelissaria was where tanners once worked, and Peyroleria was home to metal workers.

The local *auberge*, a delightfully decorated building, provides part of the unmissable pleasures of life. The panorama is wonderful and the food exquisitely simple, with genuine local dishes, such as freshly caught trout cooked with vin de Cahors, Quercy lamb from a nearby farm and a warm cabécou salad, featuring tasty local goat's milk cheese. Home of artists and writers

Saint-Cirq-Lapopie, so at one with the rocky escarpment on which it perches over the river Lot, has the justified reputation of being the most beautiful village in France.

such as André Breton and Henri Martin, and artisans who today still work in the old workshops of their predecessors, St-Cirq-Lapopie is for many *the* most beautiful village of France.

The winding road east towards the scented garrigue of the *causses* (see page 123) is shaded with chestnut and beech trees; nothing indicates that a village hides here until, suddenly, Conques appears, huddled around its cathedral on the sunny side of the river Dourdou.

Arriving in Conques, it is difficult, at first, to imagine that this abbey built in the middle of nowhere was the rival of Cluny and that, when Spain was wresting its land from the Moors and re-establishing Christian rule, abbots from Conques were in demand over the Pyrenees, in Aragon and Navarra.

There is a timeless charm to Saint-Cirq-Lapopie's higgledy-piggledy rooftops and ancient streets (left and centre), some bearing names of ancient trades. It has attracted a population of interesting artists and the French surrealist author André Breton wrote in the dovecot of the Auberge des Mariniers.

Pilgrims following the Via Podiensis on their way to Santiago de Compostela from Le Puy stopped at Conques. Ushered into the great cathedral, their eyes – and no doubt their consciences – would have been caught by the vivid depiction of the Last Judgement carved on the tympanum above the door. This rare surviving masterpiece of Languedocian art has great appeal in the naïve strength of both its style and message. Pilgrims would have immediately appreciated, for example, the scene of the weighing of souls, in which the devil is

seen to cheat by putting a finger on the scales.

The most moving testimony of this splendour of religious vocation is without doubt the reliquary statue of Sainte Foy sitting majestically on a throne. Her silver crown is magnificent, although the rather androgynous face of the saint has an almost pagan look – explained by the fact that it is now known that the face was borrowed from the statue of a young Roman emperor.

But Conques is not only an abbey, it is also a village whose history is inextricably linked with that of pilgrimage. From the Porte de la Vinzelle, the main street follows the pilgrims' route towards the Pont Romain – not a Roman Bridge at all, but a corruption of the Occitan *roumi*, pilgrim. Above a door, the sight of a scallop shell engraved on a lintel is a further reminder of the pilgrim past.

The architecture is rural and elegant at the same time. Step under the archway of the Porte du Barry, and the little lane beyond is heart-stoppingly picturesque, with pink cottages peeking out from below long, swooping roofs of grey schist. Some of the houses have two entrances, one which opens on to the lower road, the other on to the upper road or a leafy terraced garden, which makes the people of Conques say that one enters the house by the cellar and comes out by the attic. From a distance, abbey and houses merge into one, the silvery pink of the walls blending into the grey of the roofs, the cobbled streets imperceptibly becoming the rock of the surrounding landscape. Here, past and present coexist in harmony and it is unsurprising to find that Conques is an international centre for medieval art and each summer has festivities devoted to the music and art of the Middle Ages.

The three bell towers of the abbey of Sainte-Foy are a reminder that Conques was a major pilgrim halt on the road to Santiago de Compostela.

To visit Conques may be an act of devotion or an artistic pilgrimage. The church is one of the jewels of Romanesque architecture and the relics of Sainte Foy, saved from heretics during the French Revolution, are among the most precious religious treasures in France.

Along its main street, the rue Charlemagne, or any of its narrow alleys, Conques is a harmonious combination of grey and soft pink. Under a medley of grey schist roofs the weathered half-timbering is brightened only by summer flowers.

The Via Podiensis, the medieval pilgrims' route, ran from Le Puy in the Massif Central west into Spain. Here at Estaing the bridge across the Lot, like many other bridges in the region, was built for the pilgrims by an order of monks known as the Frères Pontifs.

Upstream from Conques, the long gorge of the river Dourdou joins the Lot, which flows dramatically encased between forest and heather, past Entraygues and the village of Estaing.

The first thing one sees about Estaing is the enormous castle, home of the illustrious d'Estaing family who ruled the Rouergue for more than 600 years. As you approach the river, the castle's polygonal keep and Gothic stone bridge are reflected in the limpid waters of the Lot. The backdrop of oaks, beech and chestnut trees emphasizes the colours and textures of this splendid medieval village.

Built mainly during the fifteenth and seventeenth centuries, castle and houses are made of judiciously chosen local building materials: limestone, schist, red granite from Sebrazac, flint and wood. The village is a maze of narrow streets lined with houses where roofs and façades differ in style. The older houses carry delightful first-floor wooden balconies covered by rounded tiles. Small stone bridges covered with fern span the Caussane, a brook

which tumbles down to join the Lot in the village. At the centre, there are some remark-able *hôtels particuliers*, town houses which belonged to grander local families – the Maison Cairon, now the town hall, has a distinctive Renaissance corner turret with a pointed roof.

Each July, on the first Sunday of the month, a very ancient procession, the Saint-Fleuret, takes the inhabitants in fancy dress through the village streets. At the front of the cortège is the figurehead of the village, the archbishop of Clermont who died in Estaing in 621. He is followed by all the members of the d'Estaing family, including Tristan who saved Philippe-Auguste, the king of France who sailed with Richard the Lionheart on the third crusade, and also the admiral d'Estaing, who commanded the French fleet in the decisive naval battle of Saintes, during the American War of Independence. The feasting that follows is an opportunity to taste very local cheeses: the cabécou d'Entraygues and a delicious small ewe's milk cheese from nearby Espalion. Also on offer will undoubtedly be the irresistible *fouace*,

Ambialet's Benedictine priory, perched on a rock on the left bank of the Tarn, can only be reached on foot, but the reward is outstanding views of the meandering river and breathtaking landscape.

(overleaf) South of Conques lies a land of secret charms, where the dark woods yield treasures like truffles, chestnuts and walnuts.

a glazed golden brioche, and *tarte encalat*, the speciality baked cheese tart of the area. Vin d'Estaing, a real *vin du pays*, is excellent, whether red or white.

A large lazy circle south brings you to the banks of the Tarn. The most visited Tarn Gorge villages are further upstream (see page 127), but Ambialet is exquisite. Following the river from Saint-Juéry near the famous waterfall of the Saut-du-Tarn, Ambialet suddenly appears, its two promontories at this narrowest stretch of the river each crowned by a church. After crossing the Tarn by the old stone bridge, the route up through the village begins by a most unusual gate of an abandoned farm hidden among the oaks and chestnuts. The atmosphere of the village is secluded, secretive, like a place dreamt about but never believed to exist in reality. Visiting Ambialet is not a leisurely affair, for by the time you have reached the bare eleventh-century Romanesque chapel at the top, visited the missionary museum in the priory and discovered l'Auder, a tree believed to have been brought back from the Holy Land by a pilgrim, you realize just how steep a gorge village can be!

On the border between the two old provinces of the Quercy and the Rouergue, perched high on a narrow promontory over a large loop of the river Aveyron, Najac and its proud ruined castle stand among striking green oak surroundings.

Overlooking dramatic gorges of the Aveyron, Najac (opposite) is an elongated village dominated by a ruined fortress which counted among the masterpieces of medieval military architecture.

Downriver from Najac, Bruniquel (right) dates back in parts to the twelfth century. The Porte Méjane is one of three surviving medieval gateways.

The castle is a masterpiece of military architecture and through history has suffered many upheavals. First built by Raymond IV, Comte de Toulouse, it was then rebuilt in 1253 by Alphonse de Poitiers, brother of the sainted King Louis. It was in English hands for thirty years between 1362 and 1390, then, during the French Revolution, was sold and the site exploited as a quarry until 1820. The vestiges of some of the outer defence walls remain, as well as the keep with its circular crenellated tower. From here the vista down on to the Aveyron valley is magnificent.

The original medieval village has almost disappeared – only one house dating back to the early fourteenth century remains. It has narrow mullioned windows, random rubble walls with rough lime jointing and an unusually short granite battlemented turret.

The Najac which today stretches along the single main street towards the east of the promontory was, at one time, the suburbs of the old village. Houses built from the fifteenth century onwards survive and, towards the centre of the village, there is a large fountain carved out of a granite monolith. Dating from 1344, it bears the coat-of-arms of Blanche de Castille, mother of Saint Louis and Alphonse de Poitiers. The street ends on a square; a typical feature of the region, it is surrounded by arcades. Here, Rabelais is supposed to have feasted on local smoked ham, the *jambon de Najac*, which is still a speciality of the region.

Although it is not immediately apparent, Najac is, in part, a *bastide* town. Founded mostly in the thirteenth century, *bastides* were model new towns of the Middle Ages, designed to build up communities – and to supply a body of fighting men when needed – in the sparsely populated south-west. Unlike other towns and villages of the period, they adhered to a planned grid of streets, and a noticeable feature was the large market place with covered arcades around the sides. Although fortifications were included in the master plan, not all were impregnable, but around three hundred survive intact between here and the Pyrenees.

The *bastide* plan had to undergo major adaptations to fit Najac's long cliff-edge site, but the arcaded square at the eastern end of the village is instantly recognizable, and an appealing place in which to sit and watch the world go by on a sunny afternoon.

Cordes, just north of Albi, is a much more typical *bastide*. Its easily defended narrow gateways and well-preserved market place, are claimed to be one of the first to be laid out. Founded in 1222 by the Comte de Toulouse as a strategic stronghold, Cordes's cliff-top position has earned it the nickname of Cordes-sur-Ciel. The principle for the layout of Cordes was inspired by the Andalucian city of Córdoba. Like its more famous Spanish counterpart, its early prosperity came from the fine reputation of its leatherwork, and several magnificent medieval houses, such as the Maison du Grand Fauconnier and the Maison du Grand Ecuyer, contribute to the finest collection of Gothic ribbed vaulting in France.

On the very edge of the gorge of the river Aveyron, a sharp rock stands against the sky. At first it is difficult to make out the castle that also clings there, almost part of the rock, as if they had grown together. Below, like a cluster of toadstools, the tiny medieval village of Penne clings to the slopes of the promontory among wooded hills overlooking the flowery banks of the river.

Penne is a jewel, with ancient flat roofs, tall, narrow houses which huddle against one another, a twelfth-century church with an octagonal apse and a pretty churchyard. From the church square, there is a good view down to the river below. Facing the church is a corner house built between two long jetties of half-timbered houses. The charm of the architecture

is due to the extreme simplicity with which the village was obviously put together. The timbering, plain or patterned, is characteristic of the region, and behind the fortified doorways, old stone stairways lead to the top of the house. The village is unspoilt, bucolic, totally charming.

On the 100 m-high cliff which dominates the confluence of the Vere with the Aveyron, stands the ancient tower of Brunehaut, which gave its name to the village of Bruniquel below. There was a time when Bruniquel was home to dynasties of noble Protestant gentlemen glass-makers, a *métier* which was not considered degrading by the French nobility. The Revocation of the Edict of Nantes, which chased the Protestants from France in 1683, brought an end to the artistic trade of the beautiful bluish glass, as the craftsmen fled the country, taking their manufacturing secret with them. Later

The little bastide town of Cordes (opposite) *is built on a rocky outcrop known in langue d'oc, the language of the south, as a* puech. *This elevated position has lent it the soubriquet of Cordes-sur-Ciel.*

Haggling over poultry and eggs in Villefranche-de-Rouergue market becomes a study in blue in the monochromatic light of early morning. The market, set up weekly in the old bastide's *arcaded square, is attended by farmers and smallholders from all the villages around.*

The mist lifts slowly from the deep valley of the Aveyron. Like a spectre from the past, the ruins of Penne castle stand watch over its shadowy cluster of ancient houses.

103

villagers made their living growing grapes, hemp for cloth and that most prized spice, saffron.

The old village on the slope of the Vère valley offers a splendid and rare collection of medieval houses. Of the three gateways that remain, one of them, the Porte Méjane, is crowned by a fine campanile and a pretty clock. Inside, it is easy to picture how prosperous this village must have been. Among the modest abodes that line the narrow stony streets are majestic houses, with splendid staircases.

West of Bruniquel stretches the Forêt de Grésigne, a large forest of oak and hornbeam with broad avenues and bridges built under Colbert, Louis XIV's finance minister, to secure the wood for the building of ships for the French fleet in the seventeenth century.

Down a winding road and, this time, it is the fortress of Puycelci which is perched on a verdant hill. In the thirteenth century it was a protective bastion for the inhabitants of the Vère river valley, and parts of the ramparts still remain. Within the walls are some surviving Gothic houses such as Maison Féral, which has a remarkable fifteenth-century chimney.

Between Bruniquel and Penne, Puycelci (above) *is one of a string of original medieval villages. Built high on a plateau overlooking the Vère valley, Puycelci looks out over the immense forest of Grésigne.*

A huge square tower rises up from the castle ruins at Belcastel (opposite), *on the Aveyron near Villefranche-de-Rouergue.*

GASCONY AND THE PYRENEES

‘The name of some regions give pleasure to read, write or pronounce. They evoke beauty, colour, music. I find the word “Pyrénées” particularly melodious... [evocative of] the flowing lines of the mountains, the gracious figure of the princess who started the legend of the region.’

This is how Jean-Louis Vaudoyer of the Académie Française described France’s most southerly mountain range, stretching elegantly across 300 km from the Atlantic to the Mediterranean. And the legend? This is the story of the beautiful Pyrene, who was seduced by Hercules and ran away from her angry father, the barbaric King Bebrycius, only to be savaged by wild beasts in the mountains. Hercules buried her on a mountain summit with these words: ‘My dear Pyrene, so that your name will always be remembered by those who will occupy this land, these mountains in which you now sleep for eternity will henceforth be called the Pyrenees.’

Approaching the Pyrenees, there is no abruptness, as in the Alps; rather, they unfold gently from the foothills to the peaks, from the warm, colourful shores of the Mediterranean with the snow-capped Mont Canigou as back-drop to the well-watered green of that most individual corner of France, the Basque country. High in the mountains there are ski resorts and spas such as Cauterets and Ax-les-Thermes, and a protected national park where enormous birds of prey glide on the thermals above the *isard*, the indigenous mountain goat, and the bear (yes, there are still a few). In between are historic towns such as Perpignan, dominated by the Palace of the Kings of Majorca, Foix, famous for its fairs, and that most perfectly conserved of medieval walled towns, Carcassonne.

Pau was the birthplace of the Duc de Navarre, who changed religion to be crowned as Henri IV, finally uniting a France which had been torn apart by warring factions and vicious religious persecution. Faith has left its mark on the region in several forms. Toulouse’s great Romanesque cathedral – the biggest in Europe – was a principal gathering point for pilgrims to Santiago de Compostela setting off on their daunting journey across the Pyrenees. Further along the route to Spain lies Saint-Bertrand-de-Comminges with, not far away, the site of a miraculous vision. When 14-year-old girl Bernadette Soubirous divulged the curative powers of the spring at Lourdes, the fate of her town was to become the destination of several million faithful each year. And who could forget

and the great number of fortified hill villages scattered across the landscape tell of the region's unsettled past. From a distance they can be seen set on an isolated outcrop or clinging to the rockface, their tall houses huddled together around the vestiges of a fort or a church. Their charm comes from the simplicity of the architecture, as, for speed and security, local stone and good mortar were simply used.

To reach the western Pyrenees, you must first cross Gascony. Gascony, Gascogne, may no longer officially exist, but it is a name which conjures up powerful, and pleasing, images – of foie gras, fine armagnac and that dashing, ever-optimistic friend of the Three Musketeers, d'Artagnan. This far south, fields of tobacco are a common sight, and much gossiping is done, along with the knitting and mending, on verandahs strung with drying tobacco leaves and ears of sweetcorn.

Larressingle is a testimony to the troubled times of medieval Gascony. Hollyhocks and wild flowers fringe the houses which form part of the ramparts of this thirteenth-century fortified village. The castle, of traditional regional style,

The pocket-handkerchief citadel of Larressingle (above and opposite) is known as the Carcassonne of the Gers. This tiny fortified village, with its crenellated turrets and ramparts, was never attacked and remains intact like a scale model of military architecture.

the thirteenth-century massacres of the Cathars, hounded to death in their mountain-top retreats by the cruel Simon de Montfort.

The size of the castles – some, like Larressingle, almost self-contained villages –

(page 106) Encircled by the vineyards of the Côtes du Haut-Roussillon, the small village of Castelnou, near Perpignan, was a stronghold against the kings of Spain. In the background, majestic against the clouds, is the area's highest peak, Mont Canigou.

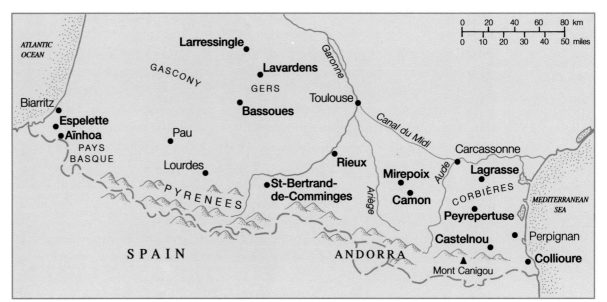

the main residence of the abbots and bishops of Condom, was torn apart by Anglo-French and religious wars. The ruined fortress was acquired as a national asset after the French Revolution and Larressingle is unique being the smallest inhabited fortified village in France. It is also one of the most endearing small villages found in the Gers.

At the heart of Gascony, the Gers countryside is a succession of pale golden knolls and open plains given over to the culture of cereal crops. Overlooking this fertile land is Lavardens. Dominated by an enormous castle which once belonged to the Comtes d'Armagnac, its tall rubblestone walls rise from the hill it occupies, flanked by two gigantic square corbelled towers. The castle's stone entrance staircase has been partly carved out of the rock face itself. Concerts and art exhibitions held in the immense rooms have given the old fortress a new lease of life.

The village, beside its pair of large lakes, has a peaceful, southern look, the low, modest houses with their thick rounded roof tiles merging with the warm colours of the country-side. On the south side of the village many of the houses have long open galleries, a handsome vernacular detail for a very practical reason: in this agricultural community fruit and vegetables are put out here during the summer to dry.

Not far away another village crowns the crest of its hill with an imposing wall bristling with fortifications. Passing through the massive gateway into Bassoues and along the main street brings you to a splendid *couvert*, the arcaded market place that typifies a *bastide*. The elaborate wooden balconies and timbering

Standing proud on a rocky promontory, the unusual château of Lavardens (left and top right) dates back to the Middle Ages but was rebuilt in the seventeenth century. The church's strong porch and campanile were built from one of the château's original towers.

on the houses reflect a certain prosperity, but the machicolations on the tall keep, through which boulders or other weapons could be rained down on assailants, are a reminder that for much of its history it was the army, not architects, who shaped Bassoues.

Tucked away in the western limit of the Pyrenees, and straddling the border with Spain, is the domain of the fiercely independent Basques. Their language, Euskara, has its source outside Indo-European roots and their history and traditions are quite separate from the rest of France. Ironically, the beret, which says 'Frenchman' to all foreigners, is actually part of Basque dress. The Basques are Basque before being French, and shutters and doorways in the neatly manicured villages are painted the colours of the Basque flag: red and green.

Inland from the cosmopolitan crowds of Biarritz, Aïnhoa is typical of the villages of the Labourd, one of the three small provinces of the Basque country. The brightness of these villages among the rich green pastureland comes almost

Bassoue's powerful fourteenth-century tower (below) is a local landmark. Pretty cobbled streets and half-timbered houses spread out from a large covered market.

Once on the mule drivers' road from Bayonne to Pamplona, the village of Aïnhoa, near Saint-Jean-de-Luz, prospered in the seventeenth and eighteenth centuries. Its white houses and freshly painted red and green woodwork are archetypical characteristics of a Basque village.

as a shock after the soft stone and weathered wood of the rest of the south-west. *Etche*, the house, is the bastion of the family and always extremely well looked after. In the Labourd region carvings and inscriptions on the white façades are repainted each midsummer, on Saint John's Day.

Beside the simple red-stone church in Aïnhoa, as in every other Basque village, is the tall bare wall, the *fronton*, against which are played the

endless games of pelota, the Basque national sport. Tradition here is not something to be put on for the tourists, but an integral part of daily life, and private lives are lived behind closed doors, not acted out in open-air cafés.

Near the Spanish border and high above the Bay of Biscay, Espelette is an old feudal village built around the church, the *auberge* and the inevitable *fronton* wall. But what first catches the eye on entering Espelette are the red peppers. They seem to pop up at every turn: strings of peppers set out to dry hang like necklaces on every house wall, every balcony; they are bargained over at the lively twice-weekly market, are celebrated in an annual festival each autumn and, of course, they figure daily on the menu of the *auberge*, as *pimientos del piquillo de Lodosa*. The magnificent *auberge* is also the place to sample Madiran, which is the excellent wine of the region, for it does not travel well.

South of Toulouse, Saint-Bertrand-de-Comminges is sometimes called the Mont-Saint-Michel des Terres because, like the famous mount in Normandy, it is built on a lone outcrop of rock around a twelfth-century cathedral. This was once the fortified Roman city of Lugdunum Convenarum and excavations, which can be visited, have already uncovered the ruins of the

forum, the theatre and spa built around 72 BC.

A local legend says that on some winter days you can see, set in the ice of the pond, the head of Salome. The tale may have arisen because Salome's stepfather, Herod Antipas, is said to have been exiled here (or perhaps to a greater Lugdunum, Lyon) after Christ's crucifixion. More probably the legend grew around a lost consignment of ice. The men of Comminges, who traded in blocks of ice, would bring them down from the mountain tops swathed in hemp sacks, protecting their shoulders with a sheepskin.

The Roman city fell to invaders from the east in the sixth century, and it was Bertrand, Archbishop of Comminges in 1033, who started building today's cathedral. Another Bertrand, Bertrand de Got, who completed the work started by his predecessor, later became Pope Clement V.

To experience the essence of the little town, pass through remains of the barbican, under the Porte Cabirole, and stroll along a street lined with medieval houses to the cathedral. A major

Known as the Mont-Saint-Michel des Terres, the cathedral and village of Saint-Bertrand-de-Comminges (above) *cling together on their hillock surrounded by a sea of green. In the foreground is the church of Saint-Just, in the neighbouring village of Valcabrère.*

The tiered bell tower on Aïnhoa's church (left) *is typical of the Basque country. Inside is a very ornate painted ceiling and, an unusual sight, the Stations of the Cross depicted on ceramic tiles.*

Row after row of red chillies are hung out to dry along the south-facing walls and balconies in Espelette. This feudal village is today a very traditional Basque community, where feast days and festivals are celebrated as they have been for centuries, and the graves in the cemetery are marked with the unusually shaped Basque headstones.

stopping point on the pilgrim route to Spain, the religious aspect of Saint-Bertrand was continuously added to and embellished. The cathedral's Romanesque portal, with a tympanum above representing the Madonna and Child and the Adoration of the Magi, leads into the large, southern Gothic nave. The pride of the church is its sixteenth-century organ, decorated with country scenes and mythologic representations and held at a curious angle by five Corinthian columns. To listen to an organ concert here, seated in one of the beautifully carved oak stalls, is spiritually uplifting. Even more entrancing is to stand in the graceful open cloisters and contemplate the peace and beauty of the valley below.

Halfway between Saint-Bertrand-de-Comminges and Toulouse is the fine medieval village of Rieux. Once an important commercial centre, with a reputation for learning – the episcopal court and law courts were set here – Rieux is now a quiet backwater beside the river Arize. The episcopal palace is still here, just off the place de la Halle, and overlooks the tall octagonal cathedral. The brick and intricately decorated woodwork of the houses reflect not only the quality of the craftsmen that Rieux attracted, but the wealth of their owners. In the Ariège of the Middle Ages, brick laid in herring-bone and diamond patterns was used to infill between the timbers, and the amount of brick used announced the wealth of the owner.

Each May, medieval Rieux is re-created, as the villagers dress up to participate in the annual festival, a noisy colourful affair involving the spectacle of local archers firing at a suspended model parrot.

Camon, a small fortified village with a large abbey-château stands on a pretty hill, among vine slopes, in a loop of the river Hers. The position on the borders of the Aude and the Ariège, was first chosen as the site of a Benedictine abbey. The archives of the region

This tall house in the village of Camon, near Mirepoix, gives commanding views over the surrounding countryside. The timbering of buildings in this region is often very elaborate, reflecting the skill of the craftsman and wealth of the owner.

To the Monday market in Mirepoix comes local produce ranging from live geese to freshly picked juniper berries and prized wild mushrooms. In autumn, pharmacies display a large pictorial chart of wild mushrooms so that people can check that the fungi they have picked are safe and good to eat.

reveal that the grandson of Charlemagne gave a donation to the monastery in the tenth century, that it escaped the Catharist heresy and was extended and embellished until a great flood destroyed it all in the thirteenth century.

Rebuilt, it played a great role in the Hundred Years War when a protective defence wall was topped by a forest of crenellations from which the enemy could be showered with arrows. The abbey was none the less ransacked and abandoned by the monks in 1494, finally to be sold as state land during the French Revolution. The Lemosy d'Aurel family bought the castle in 1848 and Dominique du Pont, their direct descendant, now lives there.

The colossal castle, with its huge square tower and a handsome double-arcaded balcony, can be visited by appointment. One can walk along the sixteenth-century ramparts and enjoy the spacious rooms. In the eighteenth-century *salons* there are pretty gypsum carvings as well as, in the Salon des Quatre Saisons, marvellous blue *camaieu* paintings. The sixteenth-century frescoes in the oratory depict the tales of Aesop. This detailed and elaborate work had been completely hidden under plaster in the eighteenth century until revealed by the present owner in 1964. The castle can be hired for receptions, when the Grand Salon is given over to the guests. Throughout the year concerts and painting exhibitions are held here.

The oak pillars supporting the couverts *in Mirepoix (left and top) each bear a carved face. These covered arcades were a feature of* bastide *towns and in Mirepoix, founded in 1279, shops still shelter beneath them.*

Lagrasse (right), which is the seat of an ancient abbey and cultural centre of the Corbière region, straddles the river Orbieu. Its two parts are linked by several bridges, and the original medieval bridge is still in use.

By the beginning of the thirteenth century, the Pyrenees were the last bastion of the Cathars. Catharism had flourished in the Languedoc, where their simple faith – the name means 'the pure' – and rejection of the pomp and trappings of papacy had attracted merchants and noblemen as well as peasants. In response they were persecuted by pope and king alike, driven to the mountains, to settle in ever more inaccessible hilltop fortresses. One of their last refuges was Peyrepertuse. This remarkable citadel, protected within 2.5 km of ramparts, perches on the very edge of a forbidding ridge – it was deemed impregnable and never attacked, and even today seems out of reach. Peyrepertuse, with Quéribus and Aguilar, was one of a chain of Cathar strongholds which included Carcassonne and, further west, Montségur and Montaillou. Cathar resistance in these remote citadels lasted almost forty years, but they were finally exterminated as heretics under the orders of Simon de Montfort.

High on a limestone ridge stands the impregnable Cathar fortress of Peyrepertuse. Below, in the village of Duilhac-sous-Peyrepertuse, villagers still recount the legend of the unfortunate Blanche of Castile, the woman in white who walks the ruin in search of her king who abandoned her 600 years ago.

In the massif de Corbières, the undulating region which, from Carcassonne to the Mediterranean, shelters the most beautiful vineyards of the south, rises the square keep and bell tower of the once-powerful Benedictine abbey of Lagrasse.

Walk through the vines, among fragrant pines and the sound of cicadae and you will reach the Pont Vieux, its perfect arch reflected in the river Orbieu. It was built in the twelfth century to link the abbey to the village, which became very prosperous and had its own church. Saint-Michel was a sanctuary built in the fourteenth century; it holds a magnificent statue of Mother and Child. Lagrasse has kept some vestiges of its medieval ramparts as well as two stone

Artists who have been attracted to Collioure include Picasso, Matisse and Braque, whose works hang in the main café in this Mediterranean fishing village.

gateways: la Porte de l'Eau and la Tour de Plaisance. The village has some remarkable houses, such as the Maison Lautier with its ornate façade painted in the sixteenth century. Parts of the village are even older, with beautifully sculptured doors or ornate ceilings. The covered market place, place de la Halle, dates from 1315. Once the commercial centre of the region and the home of rich textile merchants, some old shops in Lagrasse have been kept intact, with arched windows and antique shutters. In the place de la Bouquerie, beside a fourteenth-century house, there is a charming pink marble fountain, a cherub's face from which water spouts.

Across the bridge is the Benedictine abbey which was once the cultural centre of the region. Today it is owned by the commune of Théophanie who pass their lives quietly among the prestigious buildings they have inherited: the eleventh-century primitive chapel, the abbot's chapel with its interesting frescoes, the Salle des Gardes, and the large thirteenth-century dormitory.

Between Mont Canigou and the sea, along the picturesque road which links Céret and Collioure, lies Castelnou. The village is built on the south face of a promontory of the Aspres, at the foot of a very narrow wooded valley. It is dominated by its huge tenth-century castle, a stronghold erected as defence against the King of Aragon, just the other side of the valley.

The village's treasury of medieval houses, with their outside staircases and covered loggias, attracts many visitors and artists. The steep climb to the castle, among cedar trees and conifers, rewards with a magnificent view down over terracotta roofs and minute terraced gardens, to the vineyards that shape the surrounding landscape. Vines were first planted in this region by the Romans, and the plains of Roussillon form the most prolific vineyard in the world, with a backdrop of rocky white limestone

pungent with wild thyme and rosemary. The first olive trees and cypresses mingling among the evergreen oak and chestnut hint that the Mediterranean is near at hand.

With its seventeenth-century pepperpot church at the entrance to the small harbour, Collioure is a quaint seaside village which specializes in the salting of fresh anchovies and has an excellent sweet Banyuls wine. The unusual anchovy fishing boats lie along the old harbour, and on the sea front is an impressive fort: le château des Templiers. The church, with its pink cupola, contains nine amazing gilded altarpieces, the greatest of which was carved in 1698 by Catalan sculptor Joseph Sunyer.

Collioure inspired Matisse and the Fauvist movement and, since then, numerous artists have been drawn to this colourful place, with its spirited Catalan atmosphere.

Anchovy fishing boats leave the port at Collioure just before sunrise, lighting their path with a large round lamp, the lamparo, *placed at the front of the boat. For the women of Collioure, the salting of anchovies is still a principal activity.*

THE TARN AND ARDÈCHE GORGES

On the southern edge of the Massif Central, the landscape flattens out into arid plateaux cut by breathtaking gorges. The limestone uplands, the *causses*, are secretive and fascinating, seemingly abandoned to the scattered flocks of sheep grazing between the low stone walls of long-forsaken *bergeries*. The town of Millau, just west of the *causses*, has been a centre of fine leatherwear, particularly gloves, since the twelfth century. In the nineteenth century, there were more than twenty glove-makers in this small town and, even today, the area still provides sheepskins and fine leather for the luxurious world of French and Italian haute couture.

The gorges of the river Tarn, splitting the Causse Méjean from the Causse de Sauveterre, are about 50 km long and sometimes no wider than 50 m, and despite their obvious danger attract white-water rafting and other water-sports enthusiasts. The tortuous road which follows the gorge is dramatic in places, crossing tiny bridges and inching along narrow escarpments. The picturesque villages it passes through have their feet on the water's edge or else cling to the perilous ravines.

Upstream, past the willows and waterside cafés of pretty Florac, is the beginning of the Cévennes and the Pays de Cèze. Characterized by picturesque villages, striking medieval castles like Saint-Bonnet and le Castellas, striking cave formations such as Saint-Ambroix or Trabuc and the extraordinary Cirque de Navacelles, a natural bowl between the Causse de Blandas and the Causse du Larzac. Certain pathways, called *drailles* on maps, are the ancient drove roads used by shepherds to move their huge flocks in the transhumance, when the sheep are moved from their winter quarters in the valleys to spend the summer on the heights of the Cévennes. This barren landscape has the most beautifully scented air in the whole of France, for the scrubby undergrowth here is the *garrigue*, a bouquet garni of all the southern herbs, from thyme to wild mint. In 1879, Robert Louis Stevenson recorded his journey through this vast unspoilt region in *Travels with a Donkey in the Cévennes*.

The other great gorges of the region are formed by a tributary of the Rhône. In complete contrast to the busy commerce of the Rhône valley, the Ardèche is truly wild, with precipitate canyons, chestnut forests and ancient villages with, here and there, the reminder of an unusual crop which once boosted the economy in the region: some farmhouses are still surrounded by

(page 122) *An old Templar strong-hold, La Couvertoirade is today a very singular village, a haunt of shepherds and artists with myriad shops and interesting cafés and restaurants.*

The fortified village of Sainte-Eulalie-de-Cernon (opposite) was the headquarters of the Knights Templar. This fascinating village on the Causse du Larzac has a maze of secret tunnels.

mulberry orchards which provided leaves for the lucrative silk businesses in Lyon.

At a bend in the country road across the desert-like Causse of Larzac the fortress of La Couvertoirade suddenly appears, like some optical illusion. It was built between the twelfth and thirteenth centuries by the Knights Templars, the wealthy religious and military order founded for the protection of pilgrims to the Holy Land. (The French Templars all finished on the stake, after an iniquitous judgement under the order of Philippe le Bel of France, who banned the order at the beginning of the fourteenth century.)

La Couvertoirade has been restored with great care. Tightly huddled inside the surrounding wall, with its seven turrets, the village houses are typical of the region, lime-stone walls roofed with stone and terracotta tiles. On the ground floor, the barns where sheep were kept are now little shops and art galleries. To reach the upper floor, each house has a large stone outside staircase leading to a small entrance balcony: *lou balet*. On this floor was the main living room in which people lived, ate and slept.

In the cemetery by the church are the curious disc-shaped grave stones of the Templars,

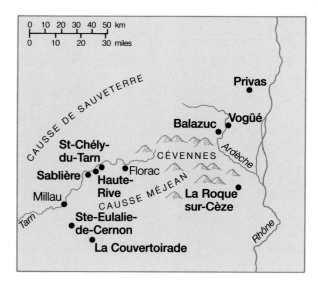

Early morning in La Couver-toirade (right). The muted sound of sheep's bells, the flock's hoofs on the dry soil and the occasional bark of a sheepdog are all part of a daily ritual which is an integral part of village life.

similar to those found in the neighbouring Laurageais, around Carcassonne. At street corners are troughs carved in the walls. These are called *conques* and were fashioned to hold drinking water for the pilgrims.

The charm of the place is retained by the rural activities which still take place. At dawn, the sheep are taken out to graze the meagre grass and herbs covering the arid surrounding plateau. Just outside the village, they will stop to drink at the *lavogne*, a large circular drinking trough with sloping slides, dug into the ground like a mini reservoir, peculiar to this area. In the evening they will be milked, and the milk kept to make the renowned blue-veined French cheese: Roquefort, which gets its name from the nearby small town of Roquefort-sur-Soulzon.

The headquarters of the Knights Templar in this area were at Sainte-Eulalie-de-Cernon, a tiny village on the Causse du Larzac. Its fortifications are still intact around a leafy square with a huge fountain and mysterious vaulted passages between stone houses.

Near the delicious little town of Florac, the Tarn gorges are a dizzying succession of cliffs and chasms. If parts of the gorges are extremely difficult to reach, the walk is easier at

Saint-Chély-du-Tarn, a gem of a village at the centre of an ancient reclaimed meander.

The small village is tucked away at the foot of sheer cliffs on the left bank of the river, and an old Roman bridge crosses to a small beach on the right bank. From here, the view of Saint-Chély is exquisite. Small cascades can be seen gushing out of the cliffs through terraced gardens and arched garden walls. The church has a square bell tower which can be reached by an outside staircase, and the old houses of the village have handsome Renaissance doors and chimney-stacks. At the centre of the village, a stream runs through the picturesque square, with the old bakehouse complete with a tiled lean-to to dry the wood, so typical of the small communities of the region. By the river, a minute chapel has been carved out of the rock face.

Not far away, the equally picturesque village of Sainte-Enimie was named after a seventh-century princess who forsook her life at court and a string of suitors to settle here and found a convent.

Pretty Saint-Chély-du-Tarn (opposite) *is one of the more accessible gorge villages, set in a natural bowl beside the river Tarn.*

Houses in the stone hamlet of Sablière (right) *are built right on the lip of the gorge. Narrow bridges and passageways link the cottages and bringing home the weekly shopping is not a simple affair when it has to be hauled across the gorge by pulley.*

The privately owned Domaine de la Croze has an enviable setting beside the Tarn. The Tarn's celebrated gorges, extremely popular despite their vertiginous drop and convoluted meanderings, were cut by the river flowing across the porous limestone of the causses. The sinuous chasm the Tarn has carved for itself runs over 500m below the level of the surrounding plateau.

In Vogüé (above), *as in many places along the Ardèche, canoeing is a popular summer recreation. Further up, in the river's deep gorges, there are excellent opportunities for white-water rafting and rock climbing.*

Balazuc's cliff-top perch (opposite) *is now appreciated by artists and artisans, rather than battle-scarred Saracens, but its ancient vaulted passageways* (right), *all sun and shadows, have changed little since medieval times.*

Travelling east, below Mont Gerbier-des-Joncs, source of the river Loire, the southern waters of the Ardèche flow past villages which begin to take on a Mediterranean feel. Vogüé, cradle of the most illustrious family of the Vivarais, les Seigneurs de Vogüé, is squeezed between the foot of a cliff and a loop in the river. Village and château have been built out of the same golden limestone and this and the round Roman tiles which cover the roofs give a distinctly southern look to the village.

This region of the Ardèche holds a surprising number of fortified hilltop villages, like the nearby feudal village of Rochecolombe. For a long time the area was racked by war and in 1427 the Vivarais was badly looted. A great number of villages also still carry the scars of the later conflicts of the Wars of Religion.

If, in Vogüé, only vestiges of the fortifications remain, the concern for defence can be seen in the way the tall, narrow houses have been built in relation to each other. To walk through the

maze of streets and the complex series of vaulted passages is to understand how easily they could be both traps to the enemy and hidden escape routes.

The village is dominated by the four towers and stout walls of the imposing château. In the courtyard, the chapel displays treasures saved from the Rochecolombe church, and from the terraced gardens it is easy to imagine this ancient village little changed in the span of five hundred years.

It is believed that the Saracens settled in Balazuc in the eighth century. Certainly, the village, perched on the top of the cliff over-looking the river Ardèche, would have made a good watchpoint in belligerent times. Built around a thirteenth-century château and a Romanesque church, Balazuc is very characteristic of the region, built in light limestone and soft pink rounded tiles, *tuiles canas*. Modest tallish houses are linked by a supporting stone arch, creating a network of shaded walks through the village streets. If, at first, the houses had been built for defence, after the eighteenth century, when people found peace, the typical pattern of country life established itself here: the ground floor, often vaulted, was used as barn to keep sheep and goats and the upper floor was the living room.

It usually had a large fireplace, in front of which the *veillée*, the evening prayers, took place at the end of each day.

Outside the village, larger, detached houses were built especially for the breeding of silkworms, a prosperous industry linked with the silk works of Lyon until the middle of the nineteenth century. The whole house, called a *magnanerie*, was devoted to the precious cocoons. Fireplaces were built at each corner of a large room to keep a constant temperature.

country road which leads south to La Roque-sur-Cèze. Well hidden, this tiny village lives on the fringe of the busy world, at the edge of the Cascades de Sautadet. Here, the river Cèze finds its way among stunning limestone formations polished and sculptured by erosion. The water is clear and to bathe here in the crushing heat of a summer's day is an invitation impossible to refuse.

To reach the village you cross the medieval Pont de Charles Martel and slowly walk among

Near La Roque-sur-Cèze the clear waters of the Cèze have eroded the limestone to form the Cascades du Sautadet (left). *The small pools are irresistible on a hot summer's day. The air here is pungent with the unmistakable scent of the* garrigue *and the resin of the pine trees which dot this stunning site.*

At cocoon time, the family left the house to the precious silkworm and took their meals on a large covered terrace, the *couradou*. The entire female population was devoted to the silkworm and it is said that the demand was such that worms were left to cocoon in the warmth of the girls' blouses.

The exquisite aroma of wild thyme, rosemary and savory floats up at every turn of the

luscious gardens, shady paths and paved streets. The houses have the simple charm of buildings solidly made with local materials by local men who know their craft.

At the top of the village you can see the vestiges of a twelfth-century château and of a chapel. A village full of nostalgic charm, La Roque-sur-Cèze is a jewel of southern architecture.

From its elevated position among vines, cypresses and maize, La Roque-sur-Cèze (right) *spreads down into the valley of the Cèze. A medieval bridge crosses the river into this photogenic village.*

PROVENCE AND THE CÔTE D'AZUR

For many, Provence *is* France – an idyll where flavours and scents are intensified by the Mediterranean sun, a land of gnarled olives and never-ending fields of soft purple lavender, a magnet for artists and lotus eaters.

But Provence is a region of huge contrasts. It is hard to believe that a few kilometres inland from the frenetic see-and-be-seen life of the fashionable coast, tiny villages have not yet yielded to sun-worshippers and the demands of an international menu.

Provence's *villages perchés*, clinging to their mountainsides, are a picturesque universe of arcaded houses and cobbled ways, labyrinths of vaulted passages and stairways, old houses squeezed together under Roman tiles faded by the sun, their narrow façades chiselled by the elements. Here and there, in shady squares, water gushes from a beautiful fountain. Only the vestiges of ramparts are reminders that these quaint villages were not built for aesthetic reasons but for protection.

Sybaritic tourists are only the latest threat to the peace of this sunny corner of France. The inaccessibility and outsized fortifications of tiny towns such as Eze and Séguret kept their people relatively safe during long periods of strife. They suffered the invasions of the fifth and sixth centuries, incursions by the Saracens and the fights and rivalry between the House of Savoie, the Comtes de Provence and the French Crown. They provided a home for heretics fleeing persecution and provided lowland villagers with temporary shelter while battles were waged on the plains below. Inhabitants of a *village perché* lived an almost self-sufficient existence, cultivating the small terraced gardens, repairing fortifications as necessary and, in times of peace, beautifying their village.

The fights have long ceased, the forts are in ruins and flowers grow by the old drawbridges. Because of their shared history, at first these *villages perchés* all look similar, but if at first it is the church, the fortress, the winding alleys of shops that attract, it is the wealth of individual detail that makes you want to return time and time again. Suddenly, you are under the spell of Provence.

Above Arles lies Les Baux-de-Provence, a formidable village built on a formidable white promontory, where history is embedded in the rock. Built by le Seigneur des Baux, who claimed to be a direct descendant of Balthazar, the ancient village and ruined castle seem to burst out of the cliffs. The effect is a calcareous chaos, a combination of erosion and excavation,

(page 134) In complete harmony with the rock on which it is built, the village of Eygalières must be the most beautiful in the Alpilles.

Fields of lavender among hills scented with wild herbs and alive with the whispering of cicadae contribute to the peaceful air that surrounds the abbey of Sénanque (right). This is the countryside that local writers such as Jean Giono depicted so vividly in their stories of Provençal communities.

at once sombre and sublime – an image worthy of Dante.

Entering Les Baux by the Porte-Mage brings you face to face with the Maison du Roi, then the Maison de Jean Brion and, further on, other fine Renaissance houses – the Hôtel de Manville (1572) is now the town hall and a museum of modern art, and the Maison Porcelet displays local archaeological finds in a vaulted room decorated with splendid frescoes.

On the corner of the Maison Porcelet is a medallion which commemorates the Provençal poet, Frédéric Mistral. It is eminently fitting that Mistral, who won the Nobel Prize for Literature in 1904, should be remembered here, for in his lyrical writing he was a direct descendant of the medieval Provençal troubadours who gathered at Les Baux, where the Cour d'Amour exemplified courtly love and romantic adventure. This peaceful, creative world was ended when the Comte de Turenne seized the town.

Access to the plateau and the castle is along rue Trencat, past remains of troglodyte homes.

From the castle ruins it is easy to appreciate the strategic position of this fort, from which the surroundings can be seen all the way down to the Camargue and the sea – an asset the Seigneurs des Baux and later the Comtes de Provence fought hard to retain. When destruction came in 1632 it was at the hands of Cardinal Richelieu, wiping out a Protestant stronghold. Only the large rectangular donjon still stands, vestige of a colossal citadel where habitation, hospital, outbuildings, cellars, dovecot and chapel have disappeared.

Although the busy visitor could purchase a guide with a title like *Les Baux in One Hour*, and rush through the village and its numerous souvenir shops, how much more pleasant and rewarding to linger in the olive groves – the source of the best olive oil of the region – enjoy the distant views and, when the evening falls, wave farewell to the last sightseer and wander through paved streets and gardens where resting warriors and troubadours once sang.

In spring, the landscape surrounding nearby Eygalières is pink with the ephemeral blossom of almond, peach and apricot trees. Unspoilt, the village stands on a crest, merging with the orchard. A defence fortification at first, the castle and church were surrounded by large patrician houses in the sixteenth and seventeenth centuries. Today it must be the most

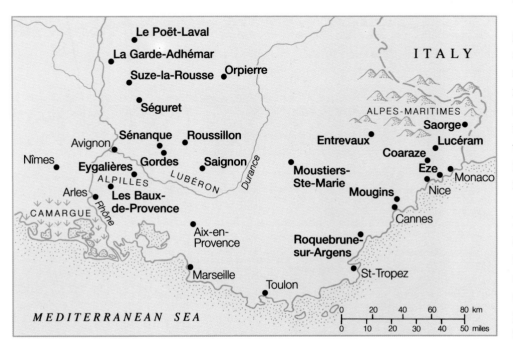

beautiful village of the Alpilles mountains. Pleasant and mellow, it overlooks olive groves, *domaines* and vineyards in this sweet-smelling countryside where the peace of the day is only broken by the happy sound of the cicadae. Just outside the village the chapel of Saint-Sixte is flanked by cypress trees, as if created by the brush strokes of Van Gogh.

In summer, as you drive towards the foot of the Lubéron, the air is filled with the pungent aroma of wild thyme and rosemary mixed with the perfume of the cedar and the maritime pine.

The roads run past myriad stone villages. Built on craggy hillsides as an early protection against invaders, their houses huddle around a church or a castle. Bonnieux, Lacoste, Saignon, Roussillon…each has its charm, its history and a charming individuality.

The *village perché* of Gordes was brought to public notice by painters such as the Op artist Victor Vasarely and Marc Chagall. Their followers, whether artists in earnest or fashionable dabblers, have made this ancient and very pretty village a 'place to be seen'.

Les Baux-de-Provence, on its bed of white bauxite, is one of the wonders of Provence. For centuries ruled by the Seigneurs des Baux, it still keeps an impassive watch over the plain below.

Nearby, the twelfth-century Cistercian monastery of Sénanque stands among lavender fields in the hollow of a ravine perfumed with all the aromatic scents of Mediterranean wild herbs. Sénanque is one of just three Cistercian abbeys in Provence – the others are Silvacane and Le Thoronet – and the monastery's stark stone stands pure and unembellished. There is a beautiful cloister where the twelve pillars supporting the arcades are crowned with finely cut capitals, each different. After a long absence, the monks have returned to Sénanque, where holy life has stood still for the past seven hundred years. To hear the Gregorian mass sung within its walls is an unforgettable and profound experience.

An unknown artist has chosen the rugged wood of this doorway (left) *to conjure up a fantasy under Italian skies. But framed in a rich terracotta hue, where else could it be but Roussillon, whose very name reflects the russet* (rousse) *and reds that distinguish the village* (left centre).

In the village, the houses reflect the shades and colours of the earth below. On one of them, there is an Italian-inspired fresco in a mixture of pastel colours complementing the terracotta mood of the village. The church is twelfth-century Romanesque and, from the *castrum*, the old hill fort, there is a dramatic view of the quarries and, in the distance, the blue Lubéron, with Mont Ventoux as a distant backdrop.

Near Apt, where deliciously prepared candied fruit have been a speciality since the fifteenth century, the village of Saignon stands on its rock like the cherry on a cake. An important seigneury in the twelfth century, it had a succession of three castles which in turn belonged to the archbishops of Apt and the Comtes de Provence. From their ruins, there are commanding views over the orchards and vineyards of the plain and the surrounding mountains.

All Saignon is a maze of flower-filled streets, punctuated by pretty squares, like the place de l'Horloge overlooked by a handsome belfry and the place de la Fontaine, with its huge fountain built in front of the arcades of the *lavoir*, where the women would come to do their washing and catch up on gossip. The place de l'Eglise, at the tip of the rock, has a gem of a Romanesque church, its naïve art coming as a surprise after the much later adornments on the exterior.

Unexpectedly, at the heart of lavender-blue Provence, a red village stands proudly at the top of a red peak, the fiery colours intensified by the deep, dark green of the surrounding holm oaks and pine trees against the blue Mediterranean sky. Roussillon, planted high on a precipitous rock, is an astonishing sight, a symphony of russets and ruby: seventeen different shades of red have been identified, created by the hydrated peroxide of iron contained in the local clay. Before the advent of synthetic dyes and paints, Roussillon was a principal source of ochre, and the spectacular quarry, a fire dance of vertiginous cliffs, deep ravines and sharp needles, bears the name of Chaussée des Géants, the giants' footstep.

In past times the fountain was the main source of water for the whole village. As Marcel Pagnol observed so beautifully in Manon des Sources, *when the village fountain dried out, life simply stopped. Fountains were often quite elaborate structures, such as in the main square in Gordes* (far left top) *and the place de la Fontaine in Saignon* (far left bottom).

In the thirteenth century, high up between two gigantic rocks above the village of Moustiers-Sainte-Marie, a huge star was born. *La cadeno*, a gold star hung on a chain, was an ex voto given to the village by the local baron of Blacas on his return from the seventh crusade. Provençal writer Frédéric Mistral sung the praises of the gold star of Moustiers and pilgrims come to make the climb to the chapel of Notre-Dame-de-Beauvoir, the delicate sanctuary below the suspended star. A special attraction, in early September, is the Messe de l'Aurore, a candlelight mass at dawn, a true Provençal affair brought to life with fifes and tambourines.

Set against a huge cliff eroded by the torrent of the Riou, Moustiers overlooks the fertile valley of the Maïre, devoted to the culture of the vine, the olive tree and cereals. It is extremely pretty, with tiny bridges linking a labyrinth of narrow streets, arcades, vaulted passages, tiny squares and reminders everywhere of Moustiers' other claim to fame: its faïence ware.

Since the seventeenth century, when the art was introduced to Pierre Clérissy by an Italian monk, the blue and white earthenware of Moustiers has been highly prized. The early pieces were elaborate reproductions of hunting scenes drawn by Antonio Tempesta, but unfortunately, the process was expensive, and by the early nineteenth century production went into a great decline. The traditional craft of the village was revived in 1925 by a local character, who named himself Marcel Provence. Poet, journalist, ceramicist, archaeologist and ethnograph, he had been steeped in Provençal culture since the age of nine. Overwhelmed by Moustiers where, for fifty years, the ceramic business had stopped, he rebuilt a wood oven and got production going again. Antique faïence de Moustiers is difficult to find, but ceramicists are all at work again, in the ancient houses squeezed along the narrow streets. The Musée de la Faïence, in a vast crypt underneath the church, retraces the history of this pretty earthenware through the seventeenth and eighteenth centuries.

Eze, perched just behind Nice, proved an impregnable refuge from the Ligurians, the Phoenicians, the Romans and the Saracens, and today the ramparts of the fortress between the sea and the Mediterranean sky are penetrated by tides of tourists eager to explore this most carefully preserved – and restored – of *villages perchés*.

Eze, le Nid d'Aigle, has attracted many artists and illustrious writers, seduced by this timeless eagle's nest: George Sand spent time here with her lover, the poet Alfred de Musset, on their way to Italy, and Friedrich Nietzsche found in Eze the inspiration for *Also Sprach Zarathustra*.

Through a fourteenth-century fortified gate, the narrow streets, stone steps and vaulted pathways are covered with heavily scented flowers and are home to artisans of all kinds, antique dealers and restaurateurs. The fourteenth-century Chapelle des Pénitents Blancs has an enamelled interior and a statue of Christ in the choir, made of dark wood, known as the Christ of the Black Plague. Higher up, the landmark of the village is no longer its castle, but the two-tier Renaissance bell tower of the main church.

Although the castle no longer exists, a unique exotic garden takes its place. Cacti and rare aromatic plants provide peaceful surroundings from which to admire an unrivalled panorama: Cap Ferrat, Saint-Tropez and, on clear days, the silhouette of Corsica.

The timid river Paillon which runs through Nice has its source just above Lucéram, the highest *village perché* of the region. On a busy Roman commercial route, it continued to be a staging post for pilgrims, *religieux* spreading their evangelical message, and other travellers.

The fortified village, with its open tower

Set below spectacular crags, Moustiers-Sainte-Marie (opposite) is the setting of a moving Provençal mass each autumn, in honour of its unusual ex voto, a giant star suspended above the village.

It is easy to get lost among the maze of alleys of medieval Lucéram (left), Provence's highest village perché.

standing dramatically against the misty landscape, shows the ingenuity used over the years by builders to make the best out of narrow locations. Some of its beautiful Gothic houses were extended by building one room over the street; these rooms, called *pontis*, little bridges, have created out of necessity an interesting maze of covered walkways through Lucéram.

High above Nice, an exotic garden on the edge of the village of Eze offers an unparallelled vista of the Côte d'Azur. Carefully restored, Eze has long been a haunt of the rich and famous.

The Baroque church of Sainte-Rosalie, like many built in Nice and the surrounding valleys has a small bulbous roof covered with varnished tiles. Just outside Lucéram, there are some interesting fifteenth-century frescoes in the chapel of Notre-Dame-de-Boncoeur, on the road to the col de Saint-Roch and also in the chapel of Saint-Grat, towards Nice, but it is in the church of Sainte-Marguerite that the treasure of the village lies. It contains four remarkable altarpieces painted between the fifteenth and sixteenth centuries dedicated to diverse saints. The masterpiece is certainly the altarpiece dedicated to the patron Saint of Lucéram, Saint Margaret of Antioch, painted by Louis Brea. Known as 'le Fra Angelico Provençal', he lived between 1458 and 1522 and was the leader of the Ecole de Nice.

In winter, Lucéram becomes an important tourist attraction for skiers who flock to the *pistes* of Peïra-Cava. In summer, these same slopes still appear snow-covered, as a magnificent ground covering of white heather comes into flower.

A spectacularly tortuous climb away from the coast and through the narrow gorge of the river Roya leads to Saorge. The landscape on the way up is grandiose and, on approaching the village, the first bulbous religious roof of this exceptional site appears. Set halfway up the mountain in a natural amphitheatre, yet only a few kilometres from the sea, Saorge was a strategic town in the Middle Ages and developed in the seventeenth century.

Siesta time in Coaraze (left): *south-facing windows will have been shuttered against the sun, while washing hangs out to dry on a wrought-iron balcony.*

Saorge (opposite) *glows in the spring sunshine and yet, in the background, the snow is still glistening on the peaks of the Alpes-Maritimes.*

Looking down on Entrevaux (left) from its fortress, the river Var seems to hold the village in check. From below, Vauban's ingenious defence strategem for Entrevaux (right) can be fully appreciated. The zigzagging wall, completing the protection afforded by the fortress, the river and the hill itself, made Entrevaux one of seventeenth-century France's strongest fortifications.

Today, calm and sleepy, the village leaves its narrow covered streets and stepways to the summer visitor. The influence of Piedmont just over the border is noticeable in the ornate houses, squeezed together as if taking mutual comfort against the overwhelming landscape. The Italian-looking Baroque church, rebuilt after a fire in the seventeenth century, is just one of the admirable religious buildings for which Saorge is noted. Like Lucéram, Saorge was a convenient stopping-off point for travellers, both religious and secular, making the long journey north or south. It became a base for several religious orders and at one time boasted twenty-five lawyers. The chapels of Saint-Jacques, Saint-Charles and Saint-Sebastian were all built by charitable organizations. There is a Franciscan convent here, too, with beautiful furniture and scenes depicting the life of Saint Francis of Assisi. To finish a visit to this pious village, stroll towards the sanctuary dedicated to the del Poggio Madonna. Its architecture, as well as the walls painted by Jean Balaison in 1480, are extremely beautiful. Behind the village there are some delightful walks to be made along paths where the rock rose and saxifrage grow wild.

In a loop of the river Var, where trout jump freely over white pebbles in the clear water, southern aridity gives way to silvan slopes and the terrain rises into the foothills of the Alpes-Maritimes. The village of Entrevaux appears, apparently on a pyramid, and linked to a fortress by a zigzagging wall and countless gateways. Is this another place of pilgrimage? No, it is a post of military defence dreamed up by Louis XIV's brilliant and innovative military engineer, Sébastien de Vauban. The strategic position of Entrevaux, its back hard up against the Alps, made it one of France's most fortified points in the seventeenth century. Three massive gateways were built: the Porte Royale, the Porte de France and the Porte d'Italie. A square crenellated donjon was added to the cathedral and, finally, an impregnable fort at the tip of the rock, linked by the wall and bastions we see today.

Since 1860, when the village was annexed to the Comté de Nice, Entrevaux has become a peaceful village with an exceptional heritage. The cathedral is magnificent, with pure Gothic vaults, deep blue painted ceilings, a gilded choir and choir stalls in carved horse chestnut.

The main drawbridge to the oval fortified village is still intact, leading through to a series of entrancing narrow alleys and stairways. The houses are all rendered in soft ochre and the outermost ones form part of the ramparts themselves. Some have an open south-facing attic particular to the region: the *soliaïré*. It is here, under cover but well-aired, that fruit and vegetables are stored and washing is hung.

The zigzag path leading to the top of the citadel is strewn with wild rockery plants, and four wonderful medieval gardens have been planted. One is reserved for poisonous plants, another devoted to aromatic plants, a third to vegetables and a fourth to fruit trees.

Along the road, now a Route Touristique, used by the Princes d' Orange to visit their *seigneuries*, Orpierre stretches peacefully along the meandering Céans river, full of genuine Mediterranean charm. Here the Provençaux play pétanque and drink pastis in the village square with the keen *alpinistes* who come to climb the surrounding peaks, such as Quiquillon, 1025 m high.

Devastated by the religious wars of the sixteenth century, the village still retains some appealing buildings of the past. From the fortified Portail du Levant to the Porte du Rochas, the Grande Rue is lined with some handsome houses with sculptured façades and beautiful doorways. The house of the Princes d'Orange dates from the fifteenth century. The

In the hills above Cannes, the little Epicerie du Centre in Mougins offers all the gastronomic delights of Provence. Above the shop, a pair of old Mediterranean shutters, jalousies, filter just enough light yet keep the room behind cool and airy during the hot months of summer.

Jewish quarter is amazingly intricate, with vaulted passages and extremely narrow lanes. It dates from the fourteenth century, when the Avignon popes decreed a Jewish enclave be recognized at Orpierre.

The sun is setting on the imposing medieval fortress at Suze-la-Rousse. Its round towers gleam, bright orange in the vine-clad surrounding landscape. Once the shooting lodge of the Princes d' Orange, the château is now the wine university.

To get to this heaven of Bacchanalian knowledge, almost, now, in the Rhône valley, one has to cross a magnificent park and a deep moat. The Louis XIII gateway leads to the inner bailey which has lost its feudal aspect to give way to elegant Renaissance crests and columns. The main stairway, restored in the nineteenth century, leads to the magnificent stuccoed dining-room and the Louis XV armoury rooms with a ceiling *à la française*. On leaving the château look at the grain market building and the old Provençal Romanesque church.

One of several fountains in Séguret (above), *this is next to an* abreuvoir, *or drinking trough. This delightful sandstone village, with far-reaching views over the Côtes du Rhône vineyards, has its own wine festival, and celebrates Christmas with a traditional* Noël Provençal *mass.*

Built by the wine and corn growers of the Argens valley to escape from the Saracens and other invaders, Roquebrune-sur-Argens (left) *is a thousand-year-old village perché with the Maures mountains as a backdrop. On the once dangerous coastline are the fashionable resorts of Saint-Tropez and Saint-Raphaël.*

The santons (opposite) *have become a Christmas tradition in Provence. These delightful figurines are of Italian origin but began to appear in Provençal nativity scenes in the eighteenth century. Early* santons *('little saints' in Provençal) were made out of wood or papier mâché, but during the French Revolution a local potter started to make* santons *in clay. They are shown gathering round the manger and represent the villagers and tradesmen who came to give their offerings to the new-born Jesus: fishermen, shepherds, gypsies, beggars, old women, maids and valets are all represented. Today they are sold in various sizes, either painted or dressed in Provençal regional costume.*

The ritual of choosing a melon: under the shade of plane trees, the air of a Provençal market (right) is full of the rich aroma of sun-ripened fruit and the strong southern accents of traders and customers.

In the foothills of the Hautes-Alpes, near Sisteron, Orpierre (left) is a paradise for hikers and climbers. Seen from Mont Quiquillon, it looks dramatically sunken into its valley. In the fourteenth century Orpierre was declared a Jewish enclave, at a time when religious persecution was widespread.

Suze-la-Rousse (above) was once a hunting ground for the Princes d'Orange. Encircled by vines, it nowadays attracts oenophiles, since a university of wine has been installed in the elegant château.

The village perché of La Garde-Adhémar (right), in the Drôme region of upper Provence, is renowned for its butterfly-filled herb garden, where some 200 types of aromatic plants are cultivated.

A crusaders' retreat in the twelfth century, Le Poët-Laval (far right) has been reborn as a centre for weaving, ceramics and other crafts.

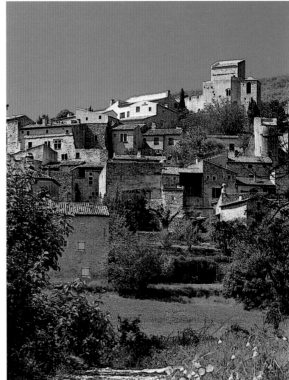

Unbroken ranks of lavender in the Drôme, just before it is picked in July (opposite). Playing its part in the economy of the region, the sweet-smelling harvest will be sold to the rich perfume houses of Grasse on the French Riviera, added to sachets of herbes de Provence, dried to perfume linen cupboards or turned into secret local remedies.

Close by, the medieval village of La Garde-Adhémar is perched over the picturesque Val des Nymphes, with commanding views over the Rhône valley, the Vivarais and the Tricastin. It is altogether an extremely romantic place, with a sweetly aromatic herb garden containing nearly 200 species, and the home of Pauline de Simiane, grand-daughter of one of France's leading *belle-lettristes*, Madame de Sévigné. The houses and artisans' shops that line the sinuous narrow streets are typically Provençal in their warm colours and sun-baked tiles, and a tree-clad lane bordered by ancient stone walls leads to the ruins of a pretty chapel in the Val des Nymphes.

On the very northern limit of Provence, on the wooded hillside of the Poët mountain in the Drôme, stands Le Poët-Laval. As picturesque as its name, it is surrounded by a landscape of gold and purple when, as in summer, the corn and lavender fields come to full ripeness.

The old village originates from the twelfth century, when the Knights Hospitallers of St John of Jerusalem used the site as a refuge for pilgrims and staging post on the way to the crusades. Le Poët-Laval was later at the centre of bloody religious battles between Protestants and Catholics (there is even a museum of Protestantism in the Hospitallers' old *maison commune*). Its fortunes then dwindled to such an extent that by the early twentieth century it was considered abandoned and its lovely old crusader castle together with surrounding houses were unthinkingly ransacked for building materials.

A renewal of interest in the little forgotten village has resulted in a gradual rebirth since the Second World War; some of the crafts, such as weaving and pottery which made it prosperous 500 years ago, have been revived, and a new centre for the arts attracts numerous visitors once more.

FRANCHE-COMTÉ AND SAVOIE

Land of wood and woodsmen, the Franche-Comté is one of the smallest regions of France, both in size and in population, but that does not stop it being extraordinarily rich in resources.

The mountains of the Jura are covered in snow all winter, but with spring arrive the centaury and saxifrage, followed by the red Turk's cap lily and the deep blue gentian, and the immense forest comes to life. The very name derives from the *bas-Latin* for forest, *juria*, and it is the trees that have shaped the nature of the region and the lives of the people. Most species grow here and each one serves a precise purpose. Oak and pine are used for building and furniture, birch for firewood and box for pipes, crucifixes, rosaries, chessboards, tobacco boxes and other fine objects. Acacia is used for the posts which hold the vines of the western slopes and spruce for the little boxes in which the delicious local cheese, Comté and Reblochon, are packed. The *montagnon*, as the mountain man likes to call himself here, says that 'wood is the companion of life from birth to death, from the baby's cradle to the coffin, from the first toy to the old man's pipe.'

Even if the ground floor of a house is built of stone, a major part of the *montagnon*'s home is covered with wood. Small tiles cut thinly from spruce form the *tavaillons* which cover not only the roof but also the outside walls, to protect the house from wind and snow. In the Vallée du Giffre, in Haute Savoie, tradition decrees that the family mark (each family has its own) is carved above doors, on furniture and on all the wooden utensils of the house.

Furniture making is, of course, another major trade. Chairs, dressers, benches and the cases of grandfather clocks (finished by another specialist artisan of the region: the clockmaker) will usually be made of pine, and colourfully painted with flowers. In country areas the *ma*, a large coffer in which the bread dough is left to rise, doubles as a kitchen table.

Guarded by a small wooden statue of Saint Georges set in a house wall, the village of Pérouges opens its gates to visitors in search of medieval nostalgia, or perhaps just the irresistible aroma of *tarte au sucre*, the traditional sweet flat pastry which is a speciality of the village.

The village is set on a hill, with orchard-clad approaches from the flat land of the Dombes area, east of Lyon. Although not entirely contained by ramparts, the village is compact and round. Large patrician houses and more modest abodes are part of the outer wall, and

the fortified church leans heavily against the village's massive main gateway, la Porte d'En Haut. The winding cobbled streets of Pérouges are typically medieval. There are no pavements and a small rivulet runs at the centre of each street to let the water drain. The roofs overlap the façade of the houses to protect the passers-by from the rain and melting snow. Although there are some good examples of timbers with corbelling, leaded lights and deep-coloured wattle and daub, many houses are built with the local stone and soft pink bricks are used at the foot of the chimneys.

From the parapet on the town's edge, there are some splendid views of the vines, the Bugey hills and, in the far distance, beyond the vast plain of Valbonne, the river Rhône. When, on Christmas night, the bells ring out for midnight mass, the epicurean atmosphere of the fifteenth-

The large village of Pérouges is partly enclosed by circular ramparts, softened in early spring by the blossoming orchards outside its walls (page 154 and above).

Situated between Bresse, Burgundy and the Lyonnais, Pérouges was the home of wealthy wine growers and weavers, who built solid, prosperous-looking houses from the local stone (right). The cobbled rue des Rondes (opposite) is typical of the medieval feel that Pérouges has retained.

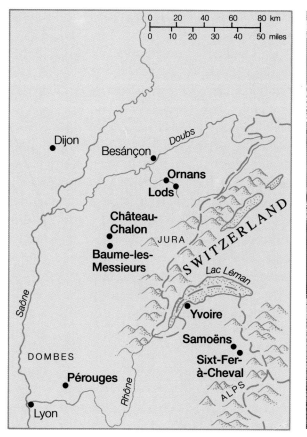

century local *auberge*, once the home of Escoffier, master of French taste, makes the little city seem to have stepped straight out of a Christmas carol.

Samoëns is a skiing village built in a valley of the Haut Faucigny, surrounded by the tall peaks of the Alps and nine pretty hamlets. The village already existed in the seventh century when it belonged to the Ducs de Savoie, but it is not until the seventeenth century that it became known as a centre for stone-cutters. Generations of masons and stone-cutters grew up and learned their trade in the area.

In 1912, skiing competitions put the village on the map again and since then Samoëns has developed into a great centre for mountain sports and walks. Around the same time, Madame Cognacq-Jay, who was born in the village, started a large botanic parkland, le Jardin de la Jaysinia. The park is at the entrance of the village, a beautiful site with cascades and home to over 4000 species of alpine plants and trees. Mountains such as the 2000 m-high Aiguille de Criou and the iced Alpine peak of Le Buet form a stunning backdrop.

The village square has a lot of style. The square bell tower dates from the twelfth century, and around the square the handsome stone houses were built by the *frahants*, members of the league of stonemasons. Over a thousand stonemasons were dispatched from here to travel through France to complete their apprenticeship. A lime tree planted in 1438 and an old *lavoir* survive, as does a covered market, built in the sixteenth century around the time when the old church, with its fine portal, was rebuilt.

A skiing resort, Sixt-Fer-à-Cheval stands in large natural amphitheatre dominated by the Tenneverge (2989 m) and the Corne de Chamois (2515 m). When the snow melts thirty or more cascades echo through the amphitheatre.

Marmots live by the water while chamois and birds of prey find their home in the huge forests which clothe the slopes.

To reach Sixt-Fer-à-Cheval, the road from Samoëns winds steeply towards the Gorge des Tines, where, way down below, the river Giffre flows. Sixt originates from 1144, when monks built a monastery here and started to clear the valley. The Gothic church and three abbey buildings from the seventeenth century survive, one serving as a hotel. The treasures from the old abbey are exhibited in a small museum. The village houses are picturesque balconied stone chalets and the large meat safes and the

well-stocked woodsheds, especially on the isolated farms, speak of necessity for self-sufficiency in the long winter months.

If you wish to eat a freshly caught perch with a vin de Crépy in medieval lakeside surroundings, make your way to Yvoire, the only fortified village of the Haute-Savoie.

Arrive by boat across Lake Geneva – Lac Léman – and you will immediately notice the defensive aspect of the place. Set at the tip of the natural promontory which separates the Petit Lac from the Grand Lac, the village is guarded by a keep and a massive fourteenth-century château. Yvoire was, in the Middle

In the hamlet of Le Mont (above), *near Sixt-Fer-à-Cheval, the snow has just started to melt, swelling the thirty torrents that drain the surrounding mountains and converge at Le Bout du Monde, a dramatic natural cul-de-sac.*

This stone and bronze fountain in the place du Gros Tilleul in Samoëns (opposite) *was built half a century ago by the village masons. The gigantic lime tree which gave its name to the square is over 500 years old.*

159

There can be fewer more peaceful scenes than this one from Yvoire (far right) looking out over Lac Léman (Lake Geneva). Yet this small village was long the focus of dispute between the houses of Savoie and Geneva, resulting in it becoming the only fortified village in Haute-Savoie.

Ages, in full control of military and commercial operations between the comtes de Genève and the Ducs de Savoie.

Yvoire today is a joy. In June, the streets are sweetly scented by wisteria, the ancient wooden balconies are adorned with bright geraniums. The delightful gardens of the château were created on the theme of the five senses by the Comtesse d'Yvoire, with a maze and an aviary set in the old *potager*. Narrow streets lead to the beautiful Baroque church with its shining metallic spire and magnificent thirteenth-century choir. Surrounded by high peaks and mountain villages, Yvoire and the lake are full of dreams and legends.

Despite its lakeside location, houses in Yvoire have inherited the pretty wooden balconies and deep roof overhangs characteristic of their mountain-dwelling neighbours (right). In a few months every available corner will be filled with a pot of flowers as Yvoire jealously guards its reputation as the foremost village fleuri of France.

When this part of Europe was still settling down, in geological terms, a stretch of what is now Franche-Comté was split open, forming a U-shaped valley surrounded by chalky cliffs. The massive subsidence was induced by erosion caused by numerous underground streams.

Six hundred years ago, an abbey was built by

Typical Franche-Comté farmhouses line the road which leads to the spectacular Cirque de Baume, a million-year-old geological formation where in the sixth century Saint Columbian came to found an abbey.

Baume-les-Messieurs was originally a monastic community where, in the sixteenth century, only noblemen could become monks. The most illustrious of these 'messieurs' was Jean de Watteville. Having killed a man in a duel, he left the brotherhood, became a Muslim with his own harem and finally found absolution in Baume, where he ruled the monks until his death.

noble monks in the middle of the site. Like village squires, they used serfs to tend the land, subjecting them to poverty and abuse while the monks lived in total luxury. With the French Revolution, things changed. The penurious folk ransacked the abbey, and burnt and destroyed every aristocratic artefact – servitude gave way to iconoclasm.

The abbey has now been divided into homes, to become the village of Baume-les-Messieurs. Mullioned windows look upon a handsome stone fountain at the centre of the courtyard, sweet-corn is hung to dry in bunches under the overlapping roofs. The sixteenth-century cloister has unfortunately disappeared, but remains are still dug up in the village from time to time. Baume-les-Messieurs is contained in its own valley like a jewel in a box. The river Seille rushes along the centre of the canyon, echoing against the high cliff walls of this valley cut off from the rest of the world, where rare flora and fauna flourish and stone spearheads lie on the floors of huge caverns.

A sharp cliff on one side, the slopes of a famous vineyard on the other side, this is the dramatic setting of the exquisite hill village of Château-Chalon. Down below the river Seille meanders, and, from the village, there are magnificent views across vines and the Jura's wooded landscape.

Despite its strategic defensive position, the village was damaged many times throughout history. A few ruins can still be seen, but what remains integrates perfectly with the surroundings. At its centre stands an eleventh-century church with a dark grey limestone roof. Around it the rural houses are an elegant mixture with red and black roofs, nicely laid-out walled gardens and ancient lime trees, all adding to the charm of the village.

But, above all, Château-Chalon is *vin jaune*. A rare wine, golden in colour, strong and very aromatic, it has a bite of walnut and honey. It is

the only French wine allowed by the EU to be sold in 62 cl bottles. The fame of *vin jaune* was assured when Napoleon, drinking wine with Metternich in Prussia, exclaimed: 'This must be the most elegant wine in the world.' To which Metternich answered: 'In this case, the best wine in the world comes from a small village of your empire: Château-Chalon.' The exceptional wine was, at the time, grown by the nuns who ran the abbey.

Today, the wine comes from a small vineyard west of the village which grows just one type of grape, the Savagnin, very similar to the Traminer of the Rhine valley. On the list of *vendanges tardives*, the grapes are not picked before early November. Once pressed, the juice is left to ferment. The following spring, it is carefully transferred to oak casks where it will be kept at least six years (some are aged in the cask for a whole century). The small bottles are

Château-Chalon, surrounded by vineyards, devotes its time to wine. Its potent, expensive vin jaune *is aged at least six years before being drunk.*

The weirs on the river Loue at Lods (opposite) were originally built to supply fast-running water to the village's blacksmiths and mills.

called *clavelins* in memory of a missionary nun, native to the region, who was martyred in Tien-Tsin in China in 1870. As a footnote, Louis Pasteur, who did much research on the fermentation with the local wines, was born in nearby Arbois.

Set by fast mountain rivers, most of the villages of the Doubs were the first industrial centres of the region. The sound of paper mills and forges echoed in the narrow valleys and on the hills, vines, orchards and kitchen gardens were planted in steps clinging to the rock behind the pitched roofed houses and church steeples tiled with *lauze*, slivers of the local limestone.

On a steep hill above the Loue valley, the ancient wooden wheels and mill-races of Lods are a legacy of France's first electrical energy,

produced with water power. The river washes the foundations of the old balconied houses. At the back, the wine grower's houses nestle along the steep streets. Built in the sixteenth and seventeenth centuries, they have huge arched cellar entrances which open directly on to the road. A few stone steps give access to the main door of the house. The façades are flat, but lintels and stone window frames are sometimes decorated with elegant arabesques or a bunch of grapes or two. Today, the vine growing of the region has disappeared, but the houses have been sympathetically restored.

The neighbouring riverside village Ornans also appeals, with its picturesque waterside location. Its unpretentious charms were immortalized on canvas by the local-born nineteenth-century artist, Gustave Courbet.

At Ornans (right) the Loue widens to form the miroir d'Ornans, *a calm stretch of water in which the wooden balconies of the old village houses are reflected. Gustave Courbet, who was born in one of these houses in 1819, painted numerous scenes of his native village, including the* miroir.

BURGUNDY

———

Only the philistine would dare pass quickly through Burgundy. For if the mere name evokes splendid wines, fine cellars and epicurean sustenance, there are so many other reasons to pay a special visit to France's oldest province.

From cavemen to dukes who, from their solidly built forts and castles, managed for centuries to remain independent from the French Crown, to illustrious clergymen who preached Christianity, won religious wars and built today's revered temples of Romanesque art, Burgundy has a wealth of history.

Geographically it is a land without natural frontiers, where the picturesque never ends. From the Champagne to Lyon and the Auvergne to the Franche-Comté, it is a fusion of small pastures and large open fields, flat land and rolling land, pitched roofs with flat tiles and flat roofs with pantiles, where spirit and *esprit* are inextricably linked. Burgundy reconciles spring water with wine, ascetism with good living, splendour with homeliness.

The many villages are picturesque and varied in style, according to their location. But the modest *maison vigneronne*, always built with its cellar beneath, is omnipresent throughout this region where grapevines are an integral part of the landscape.

In the south of the region, in an area known as Romanesque Burgundy, stone villages with their brilliant red tiles surround a Romanesque church, a *pigeonnier*, or a substantial farm with turrets and covered galleries. Semur-en-Brionnais is one of them, a pure example of the archetypal architecture of the Maconnais.

Semur-en-Brionnais stands handsomely on the crest of a hill over the rich pastureland of the Brionnais. It was the native village of Saint Hughes. Son of a local aristocrat, he was responsible for the building of the great abbey at Cluny, a name to conjure up images of powerful monks who were theologians, architects and artists.

The church is a remarkable example of twelfth-century country Romanesque art. The semi-circular arched doorway has a very heavily carved lintel, the roll moulding twisting to join the Corinthian column below. Inside, there are some splendid bas-reliefs. Beside the church is the old priory, built in the eighteenth century with material from a ruined Cistercian abbey, and on the small place de l'Eglise stands an elegantly built town hall. The school is an imposing house of the same era and, to finish the architectural balance of this unusual village square, there is a fine sixteenth-century house with a pretty round turret. Narrow beaten-earth lanes lead to the lower part of the village, where the houses are opulently rustic with beautiful gardens, local tiled roofs and stonework made out of the local sandstone.

As you leave the village through the vaulted

Madeleine gatehouse, the pretty Saint-Martin stream lingers across meadows where the white Charolais cattle graze. In nearby farms, turkeys and hens peck at the grass, and under the covers of the kitchen roofs the traditional square Burgundian cheese cages hang down from a beam.

If Salmaise is only a step away from the source of the river Seine, a look at the surrounding countryside, the hills and the geometric patterns on the roofs tell you that you have already travelled a long way from Paris. This is the Côte-d'Or, where cow pasture gives way to vineyard, and where Dijon, the capital city, allies the art of Burgundy with the art of the table.

An ancient prehistoric encampment, with a château which belonged to the Ducs de Bourgogne and became one of the most important fortresses in the region, the village of Salmaise is unspoilt and has the solid rural charm of a Burgundian village, with its medieval *halles*, covered market, *lavoirs* and fountains. The eleventh-century church rightly has its place in

The church of Saint-Hilaire in Semur-en-Brionnais (above) is a fine adaptation of the Romanesque style of Cluny to a rural church. Its architect, a native of Semur, also founded the great abbey at Cluny. Among the orchards and meadows (right) that ring Semur stands the prettiest of country chapels: Saint-Martin.

Started in 1015, the enormous fortress of Salmaise (opposite) took 300 years to complete.

(page 166) Neat rows of vines clothe the rolling Burgundian hills near Bué, in Sancerre.

the chain of Burgundian Romanesque churches, with ancient statues and a Roman ex-voto dedicated to the goddess Sequana. Walks among the rocks of the Oze valley are pleasantly refreshing and lead to the wooded site of the hermitage at Saint-Jean-de-Bonnevaux.

At the heart of glorious Burgundy, the basilica of Sainte-Madeleine in Vézelay dominates the valley of the river Cure from the top of France's *colline éternelle*. In the eleventh century, Vézelay became the pilgrimage centre of the Christian world. Not only was it the main point of assembly for journeys to Santiago de Compostela, but it was here where Saint Bernard preached the second crusade in 1146, and where Richard the Lionheart and Philippe Auguste set off for the Holy Land on the third crusade of 1190. Christian or not, the mystic aura of Vézelay is still something palpable.

Apart from its ecclesiastical and feudal buildings, Semur-en-Brionnais has some opulent houses built by the area's rich Charolais cattle breeders. Part of Semur's vernacular architecture, this summerhouse above a gateway stands beside a splendid garden. The arch leads to the chemin de ronde *that encircles the village.*

Vézelay's colline éternelle, *eternal hill, is crowned by the basilica of Sainte-Madeleine.*

Like the pilgrims of yesteryear, it is perhaps most satisfying to approach Vézelay on foot, through the vines and across the green valley of the river Cure. First stop, Pierre-Perthuis, a pocket-handkerchief community reached across a paved thirteenth-century bridge. Next, Saint-Père-sous-Vézelay has a Gothic church which is all elegance, and finally you are at Porte du Barle, the pilastered gateway to the medieval village of Vézelay. In the place du Clocher Saint-Pierre, creepers and hollyhocks grow by the steps of ancient wine-growers' cottages, a scene full of rural charm. Yet round the corner an impeccable courtyard fronts an eighteenth-century *hôtel particulier*, once the town residence of a wealthy family. In the place Borot stands a house with a corbel and turret holding a seventeenth-century clock. Push the door of the épicerie Saint-Vincent and the local spiced

ginger cake is presented in baskets lined with white cloth, like the offering of bread to the first pilgrims.

In Vézelay, nothing is obvious, everything is nuances, just like its basilica. This jewel of Christianity was erected by monks who were not only theologians but brilliant architects, craftsmen and artists. They managed to create a spiritual environment where, from matins to vespers, the light pouring through the narrow windows gave new life to the nave or the altar. The black and white vaulted nave and sculptured capitals are unanimuously considered a masterpiece of Romanesque art. Badly mutilated during the religious wars and the French Revolution, the basilica was admirably restored between 1840 and 1860 by Viollet-le-Duc. The magnificent tympanum over the entrance, which originates from 1120, presents

Vézelay's great basilica, erected by monks who were also great craftsmen and artists, is adorned with fine carving such as these apostles (opposite) *on the front porch..*

the Apostles on Ascension Day, the day of the ascent of Christ to Heaven. Christ is shown presiding over a group of apostles and followers, and the delicacy of the folds in their robes, blown by the wind to symbolize the ascent of the Holy Spirit, captures the spirituality of Vézelay.

Each spring, hundreds of swallows arrive in the large village of Noyers to take advantage of the shelter they find in the sixteen towers of the old fortifications almost encircled by a loop in

the stock of salt for the whole region.

Walk through the Porte Peinte, the ancient gateway, and you will discover a large ensemble of timber-framed houses with sculptured corbelling. Along the narrow streets, from square to square, the architecture of the Middle Ages rubs shoulders with the mullioned windows of the Renaissance and the cut sandstone of the eighteenth century. The traditional craftsmen still abound, their art matching the rustic carvings on the houses. The shady arcades of the place du Marché au Blé lead to the flamboyant Gothic church. The nearby college has a beautiful sundial on its façade and, as you leave by the Porte Verote, take a glimpse at the pretty statue of Madonna and Child: they hold grapes, symbol of fertility for the surrounding land.

If walking has induced thirst, stop at a little *auberge* and enjoy a chilled Chablis. You may

In Noyers-sur-Serein, covered passageways lead from one square to another, each blessed with the curious but evocative names they were given in the Middle Ages.

the river Serein. In the streets and small squares with extraordinary names such as the rue du Poids du Roy (Street of the King's Weight) and the place de la Petite Etape aux Vins (Square for a Short Halt for a Glass of Wine) Noyers simply seems to carry on with fifteenth-century life. The place du Marché au Blé (Corn Market Square) is not unexpected, but the place du Grenier à Sel (the Salt Loft) is explained by the fact that Noyers used to hold

The main gateway of Noyers (left)
*leads into a village which combines
medieval timbering, Renaissance
windows,* hôtels particuliers *from
the eighteenth century and
balconied façades from the nineteenth. At every turn something
survives from a different age, be it
a naïve carving of an artisan at
work* (above) *or, just outside the
village, a weatherbeaten
advertisement* (centre left). (*How
long before these old Dubonnet
advertisements fade away
altogether from the walls of
France?*)

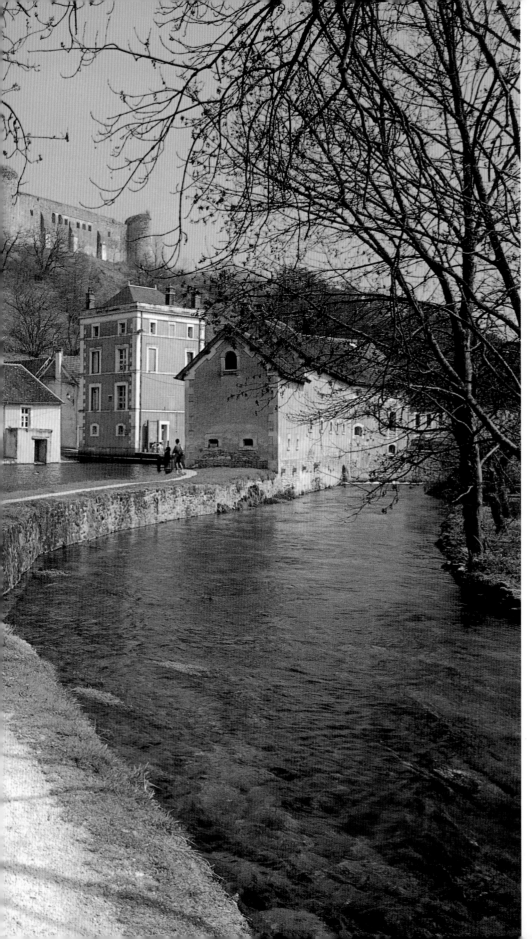

then learn from the local people some of the *chansons à boire*, those evocative Burgundian drinking songs that help spirits go high and the wine go down.

If you like mysterious places, push open the entrance gate of the château at Druyes-les-Bellefontaines, home of the Comtes d'Auxerre and Nevers, which has stood through ten centuries of turbulent French history. First in the hand of the princes of Burgundy, it became the property of the Comtes de Nevers and was finally sold to Louis de Damas, Viscomte de Druyes. From the large north tower there is a splendid view on the eighteenth-century village and the lake below.

The lake at Druyes-les-Bellesfontaines is fed by a stream which gushes from the rock face beside the fortress. This village, torn apart by war and disputes for so many centuries, is now a lovely picture of romantic serenity.

ALSACE

At Strasbourg, the capital of Alsace, there stands the magnificent pink sandstone cathedral with its Gothic spire, described by Goethe as a 'tall angel between the Vosges mountains and the river Rhine'. The surrounding prosperous region combines French and German influences, reflecting a long and sometimes turbulent political history. The Rhineland traditions here produce a unique local architectural style, best seen in the elegant and picturesque villages that dot Alsace's famous Route des Vins, a 200 km rollercoaster that swoops through the hillside vineyards.

For centuries now, the vineyards of Alsace have been the invaluable resource of the region, ruling the life and style of the many villages which are scattered along the lower slopes of the Vosges. The architecture evokes the richness of time past when, from the Middle Ages until the end of the sixteenth century, the wine-growing economy of Alsace was at its best. Many villages were then fortified and today, remains of walls, turrets and ancient gateways still surround the brightly painted houses pressed together along the winding streets, as if not to infringe upon the surrounding land.

The vernacular architecture of Alsace is original, both in shape and in colour and quite different from other parts of France. Blue, ochre and red limewash flirts with the sedate pink of the local sandstone, and elaborately carved architraves, cresting and mouldings mingle with vaulted entrance doors, oriel windows and ancient tiled roofs. The medieval and the Renaissance blend effortlessly. No other region has developed quite such a taste for the art of urban decoration: everywhere there are hand- some clocks, sundials, campaniles, elaborate house and shop signs.

La Petite Pierre, in the north of Alsace, gives a taste of things to come: the quaint eighteenth-century village houses, the characteristically intricate woodcarving around the doorways, the restaurant menus full of enticing regional dishes – La Petite Pierre is renowned as a gastronomic centre, with game, goose and freshwater fish all specialities. Adding to its appeal is the château high on the hill, once a summer residence for the local nobility, then a fortress during the reign of Louis XIV. Surrounding it is a magnificent forest in which deer are left to roam.

Perhaps the best time to travel the route is in autumn as the vine leaves begin to show their autumn colours, an extraordinary mixture of crimson and bronze. The sun-gorged grapes will soon be picked to produce such nectars as Riesling, Sylvaner or Gewürztraminer, but also Muscat, Pinot noir and Pinot gris. Weather permitting, a few bunches will be left to over-mature, until they almost rot. This *pourriture noble* – noble rotting – will give an amber wine

grower's secrets are kept behind these doors?

Seen from the vineyards Mittelbergheim looks like a mountain village, with hilly streets, no pavements and houses with unusually long and sloping roofs tiled with *Biberschwaüz* tiles. Translated as 'beaver's tail', these are flat tiles made with the local clay; ridged and rounded at the end for easy drainage. The slope is to let the snow slide off more easily. For Alsace is blessed with a true continental climate. This means that the winters are cold and harsh but they are followed by sunny springs and summers and good autumns. This climate is excellent for the quick ripening of the grapes and determines the constancy in the quality of the Alsatian wine.

The road south is magnificent: long stretches of vines, manicured villages and commanding views over the Alsatian plain and the Vosges mountains. An enlarged village, Ribeauvillé is dominated by the ruins of three castles set on the surrounding hills. They were once the property of the Ribeaupierres, powerful French aristocrats. Below, in the village, the houses are richly coloured, the winding streets fringed with

(page 178) The church spire of Niedermorschwihr rises out of an early morning mist lying over the treasured vineyards of Alsace.

The roofs of Mittelbergheim (left) *are covered with* Biberschwaüz *tiles, traditional in Alsace but seldom used any longer. The beaver-tail shape was fashioned to cope with heavy rain and snow.*

of exceptional taste and quality, sold under the appellation of Gewürztraminer vendanges tardives.

Travelling from north to south, the first major stop along the Route is Mittelbergheim. The fine spires of its two churches, one Catholic church, the other Protestant, reflect the religious and cultural heritage of the region where, in turn, French and German rule dominated. Mittelbergheim is an ancient village where craftsmanship once flourished, but its coopers, stonecutters and blacksmiths have almost disappeared. Only the wine-growers have stayed. They live in large half-timbered houses built during the sixteenth and seventeenth centuries around a rectangular courtyard complete with wine-press and barns. The entrance to the paved yard, through a magnificent portal of local pink sandstone and a huge wooden doorway, is often closed and inaccessible to the visitor. How many wine-

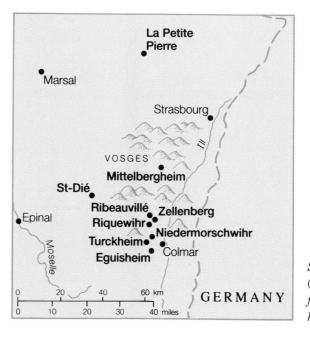

Spread out below La Petite Pierre (opposite) *is a magnificent beech forest, a reserve which is home to herds of red deer.*

artisanal and vignerons' houses two or three centuries old. There is a remarkable house with a courtyard in the Grande Rue – No 99 – a handsome Gothic church and a town hall with an interesting fifteenth-century stone balustrade. Here and there a Renaissance fountain splashes, turrets and towers sprout, such as the thirteenth century Butcher's tower which spans the main street.

Each year, as autumn approaches, Ribeauvillé prepares for Pfifferdaj, the festival of fiddlers and minstrels, a reminder of medieval times. On the Sunday which inaugurates the festival, wine flows from the fountain in front of the town hall and women and young girls wear their regional costume, with the large black bow worn at the back of the head, the *Nawelhiwala* which befits their blonde hair so well. A lot of the excellent Alsatian *charcuterie* and *choucroute*, sauerkraut, is eaten and Ribeauvillé comes alive with the colourful, noisy traditions of the past.

Cars are not allowed within the walls of Riquewihr, 'pearl of the Alsatian vineyards', built at the heart of the Schoenenbourg vineyard. Visitors are free to stroll in search of a glass of Riesling, poured from the elegant long-necked bottles used for all Alsace wines. Riesling is the oldest variety of the local wines; light and fruity, it is perfect when served deliciously chilled, accompanied by some salted *bretzel*, the dry biscuit which is a speciality of the region.

The picturesque timber-framed houses in Alsace villages are maintained with pride. Ribeauvillé (left) is overlooked by the huge castle built by the Seigneurs de Ribeaupierre, who ruled the region, while a painted shutter in Niedermorschwihr (right) recalls a more homely facet of Alsace life. Furniture, especially wardrobes, painted in this distinctive local style, was a traditional wedding gift.

Saved from the bombs of the Second World War, Riquewihr has fought twice against intrusion: once, during the thirteenth century then, much later, in the seventeenth century, when it fell into the hands of the Wurtembergs. Two separate defence walls were then built. Today, one enters Riquewihr either through the tall Dolder gateway, with its thirteenth-century belfry, or through the Obertor, an impressive crenellated inner gateway.

Well protected by such fortifications, Riquewihr proudly displays its jealously kept architectural treasures. The streets are lined with handsome bourgeois houses laced with heavily carved timbers and corner carvings, some telling the story of the house, others depicting the trade of the owner. There are softly painted shutters, oriel windows, unusual antique iron signs hanging above the doorways of wine shops. Courtyards, such as the famous cour des Cigognes, have wooden staircases and elaborate wooden balconies heavy with bright geraniums. In front of the cellars, wine-growers' carts and barrels remind the visitor that the grape-picking season is about to start, and that, for the inhabitants of Riquewihr, traditional patterns of work go on today much as they did centuries ago.

Riquewihr, amid its vineyards, is the centre for the region's wines. Caught in a time warp, it is a village where cars are banned and modern necessities such as electric cables are judiciously concealed.

185

On the Route des Vins lies
Zellenberg (opposite), *hemmed in
by neat vineyards. Like other
villages along the Route,
Zellenberg's existence is devoted
to the production of the Alsace's
fresh, clean-tasting wines.*

*Grape-picking near Turckheim:
the grapes, which are cut by hand,
are carefully placed in* tendelins,
*traditional wooden hods, for
transportation to the wine press.
From a small vineyard on the left
bank of the Fecht, Turckheim
produces an exceptional but little-
known wine called Brand.*

Above Turckheim, the mountain road is particularly spectacular and, on a sunny day, the glazed tiles of the church roof glitter in the distance. Storks nest each year over the Porte de France, the tower gateway into the village faced with a large, finely wrought sundial. Immediately beneath, a pair of lancet windows are a reminder of the time, between the fifteenth and seventeenth centuries, when Alsace was under the submission of the German reiters and mercenary lansquenets.

The wrought-iron sign over 'The Winegrower's Cradle' is one of many to be found advertising wine houses all along the Route des Vins.

At dusk a uniformed nightwatchman wishes goodnight to the villagers. In doing so, he perpetuates a tradition started in the 1500s, another example of the sense of folklore and tradition embedded in the region.

The Route des Vins ends near the village of Eguisheim, off the main road and across the river Fecht. The charmingly winding road passes the Colline des Trois Châteaux, the hamlet of Haut-Eguisheim and endless rows of glistening vines. Eguisheim, the most ancient village of the region, was the cradle of Alsace wine-growing. The noble vintages produced by the vineyards of Eguisheim were served in courts throughout Europe, and are still great favourites of the royal families of Great Britain and Holland. It was fortified as early as 1257 and remains a medieval gem, streets, colours, half-timbering and architectural details unfolding harmoniously before you as you stroll its quaint alleys.

Take a right by a corner house and you will find your way to the twelfth-century church with, above the doorway, a fine carving of Christ between St Paul and St Peter. They are surrounded by the Virgins tending the symbolic oil lamps of fidelity.

Handsome storks have again elected the bell tower as their seasonal base. Wander the narrow streets and you will discover fine courtyards, a fountain commemorating the son of a local duke who became Pope Leo IX, and the headquarters of the 'Gourmets' Association', a reminder that history, art and good living are intricately linked in this exceptionally picturesque region of France.

Turckheim's Porte de France (left) *is embellished with clock, sundial and stork's nest. In contrast to the Renaissance atmosphere of the village, Turckheim's museum organizes excellent exhibitions of modern art.*

This corner of Eguisheim (opposite) *epitomizes the storybook architecture and atmosphere of villages throughout Alsace.*

INDEX

First published in the UK 1997 by
Cassell
Wellington House
125 Strand
London
WC2R 0BB

Text copyright © Brigitte Tilleray 1997
Photography copyright © Richard Turpin 1997

The right of Brigitte Tilleray to be identified as
the author of the work has been asserted by her
in accordance with the Copyright, Designs and
Patents Act 1988

Distributed in the United States by
Sterling Publishing Co. Inc.
387 Park Avenue South
New York, NY 10016
USA

Edited by Caroline Ball
Maps by Roger Courthold

*British Library Cataloguing-in-Publication
Data*
A catalogue record for this book is available
from the British Library

ISBN 0-304-34880-5

Printed and bound by
South China Printing Co. Ltd., Hong Kong